Curry & Chilli COOKBOOK

The Confident Cooking Promise of Success

Welcome to the world of Confident Cooking, where recipes are double-tested by our team of home economists to achieve a high standard of success—and delicious results every time.

bay books

C O N T E

Black Bean Scallops in Ginger Chilli Oil, page 80

Aromatic Lamb Curry, page 50

Dry Potato and Pea Curry, page 39

Chicken and Lime Curry, page 42

N T S

Curried Beef and Vegetable Pies, page 29

Chilli Tomato Soup, page 63

The Publisher thanks the following for their assistance in the photography: Sunbeam Corporation Ltd; Kambrook; Ada's Place; Antico's Northbridge Fruitworld; Cooking Co-ordinates; Dulux Paint; Grace Brothers/Myer; Home & Garden; Huon Herbs; Live This; Narelle Derwent Ceramics; Porters Paint; Ratatak Ceramics; Steve Costi Seafood Pty Ltd, North Sydney.

Balinese Chilli Squid, page 70

Watermelon and Pineapple Salad with Jalapeno Syrup, page 73

CONFIDENT COOKING

The test kitchen where our recipes are double-tested by our team of home economists to achieve a high standard of success and delicious results every time.

When we test our recipes, we rate them for ease of preparation. The following cookery ratings are on the recipes in this book, making them easy to use and understand.

A single Cooking with Confidence symbol indicates a recipe that is simple and generally quick to make—perfect for beginners.

Two symbols indicate the need for just a little more care and a little more time.

Three symbols indicate special dishes that need more investment in time, care and patience—but the results are worth it.

Front cover: Chicken and lime curry. page 42.
Inside front cover: Fragrant Fish Curry and Curried Sweet Potato and Carrot Soup, page 31.
Back cover: Beef Vindaloo, page 23

A Cultural Adventure

Searching for unfamiliar ingredients to cook new and exciting dishes is all part of the fun when it comes to making curry or chilli. Armed with a few basic hints you will be ready to enter a world of unusual and exotic foods.

Curry and chilli—the words tickle the taste buds with a sense of warm aromas and fiery food strong enough to make the eyes water. But what exactly are these dishes that originate from mysterious and foreign climes?

Generally, we think of a curry as being of Indian origin, or at least based on dried, ground spices, as in an Indonesian Rendang. 'Chilli', meanwhile, originated in South America. Thanks to Christopher Columbus returning with the fruits from his travels, their use in cooking spread across Europe into Asia and India, so that almost every country today boasts dishes featuring some type of chilli, from Hungarian Goulash to a Creole gumbo or Szechuan soup. This is where the distinction between curries and chillies starts to become blurred. Thai curries, for example, are based on a paste of mainly fresh herbs and spices, with either red or green chillies predominating.

SPICES

The curry powders we buy in the supermarket today are derived from spice mixtures used in Indian cooking, which were copied by the British colonials on their return to England. Although not authentic, they have become so much a part of everyday cooking now in the West that it would be unthinkable not to include recipes using these mixtures.

Grind your spices the traditional way with a mortar and pestle.

Most recipes, however, ask for a combination of individual spices that will give a dish its unique flavour. Dried spices should be as fresh as possible when used, so try to buy them in small quantities and discard any past their use-by date. Ground spices lose their flavour and aroma very quickly and will contribute little to a dish, so for the very best flavour, buy whole spices and grind them yourself. A mortar and pestle is the traditional implement for this job, but you can also use a spice or coffee grinder. If using the latter, keep it specifically for grinding spices so that the coffee flavour does not permeate. Alternatively, clean it well by grinding some raw rice in it to pick up any fine residue. If a recipe asks for whole spices to be ground, and you do not have the necessary equipment, you can use an equal quantity of the ready-ground spice instead.

To clean a spice grinder, put some uncooked rice into it and grind.

Spices are usually cooked briefly, either in oil as part of the recipe (with onion and garlic, for instance), or 'dry-fried' which means you simply cook the spices alone in a frying pan, stirring occasionally, for a couple of minutes over a moderate heat. The spices will become richly aromatic when ready—take care not to overcook as they may burn and become bitter. Spices have a raw taste if not cooked at all, so if you wish to add more later in the cooking process, dry-fry them first. Garam masala is one exception, as it is often added to curries at the end of cooking. For a full glossary of curry spices, see pages 20–21.

Dry-fry spices in a frying pan, stirring occasionally, to release their aroma.

CHILLIES

The many different types of chilli have varying degrees of heat, but in general, the larger the chilli, the milder the heat. A capsicum, for example, is mild and sweet, whereas a tiny Birds Eye chilli can really pack a punch. Be aware though, that the heat and flavour can vary greatly within each type, depending on the season and locality in which it was grown, and even the age of the plant. Have a

To reduce a chilli's heat, discard the seeds and membrane before cooking.

go at experimenting with the different chillies, but always err on the side of caution—you can always add more, but you can never take it away. A good way to really taste and appreciate the flavours of chillies is to make chilli oil (recipe on page 89), using a different type of chilli each time, and eat it with some good Italian bread. For a glossary of chillies, see pages 68–69.

To lessen the heat of chillies, remove and discard their seeds and membrane with a knife before cooking. It is actually the white membrane connecting the seeds to the fruit which holds most of the fire, and not the seeds themselves, as is sometimes thought.

THAI CURRY PASTES (RED OR GREEN)

1 tablespoon coriander seeds
2 teaspoons cumin seeds
2 teaspoons dried shrimp paste
1 teaspoon black peppercorns
1 teaspoon ground nutmeg
12 large red or green chillies
1 cup (110 g/4 oz) Asian shallots, chopped
2 tablespoons oil
4 stems lemon grass (white part only), finely chopped
10 cloves garlic, chopped
2 tablespoons chopped fresh coriander roots
2 tablespoons chopped fresh coriander stems
6 kaffir lime leaves, chopped
2 teaspoons finely grated lime rind
2 teaspoons salt

1 Dry-fry the coriander and cumin seeds for 2–3 minutes, until fragrant, then grind finely in a mortar and pestle. Wrap the shrimp paste in foil and cook under a hot grill for 3 minutes; turn the package twice, using tongs.
2 Place all the ingredients in a food processor and finely chop. Refrigerate in an airtight container for up to 3 weeks, or freeze in small portions (ice cube trays are ideal) for up to 4 months. Makes about 1 cup.

Always wear rubber gloves when chopping fresh chillies to avoid burning.

When chopping fresh chillies, it is advisable to wear gloves. If this isn't possible, remember to scrub your hands thoroughly with warm soapy water when you have finished. The oils in the chilli can be extremely hot; sometimes you can even feel them burning your fingertips. If you touch your eyes (or any other delicate part of the body), the pain can be excruciating. Make sure that you also wash the knife and chopping board afterwards to avoid transferring the heat and flavour to other foods.

Roast chillies by holding them, one at a time, in an open flame.

When fresh chillies are to be added to an uncooked dish, such as a salsa, roasting them will sweeten them slightly and develop the flavour, in the same way as when roasting red capsicums. To do this, cook the chillies under a hot grill, or hold them with tongs in an open flame until the skin is black and blistered. Cool in a plastic or paper bag, or under a clean tea towel, then peel or scrape off the skins and use as directed.

Some like it hot, as the saying goes, and some like it even hotter. But never underestimate a chilli. If you realise suddenly as you chew a mouthful of food that you have been overzealous with the chilli, the best thing to do is reach for a glass of milk (not water) or have a healthy spoonful of that yoghurt raita on the table.

When the chillies are cool, peel away their blackened skins.

LOOKING FOR NEW INGREDIENTS

Most supermarkets carry a good range of chillies and spices, as well as standard curry powders. You may, however, need to visit specialist Asian grocery shops to find other ingredients, such as tamarind concentrate or dried curry leaves. Asian shops will also sell curry powders which are more authentic than the supermarket varieties. They are usually marked 'for chicken', 'for meat' or 'for seafood', making it easy for you to choose the one you need. A lot of greengrocers are now selling Asian herbs, fresh spices such as ginger, turmeric and galangal and of course Asian vegetables. If you can't see the ingredient you need, ask them to get it in for you.

Take time out to find specialist shops and explore different ethnic neighbourhoods, and don't be afraid to try something new. You may find that the desire to cook a meal can turn into a cultural adventure.

CURRIES

CHICKEN TIKKA

Preparation time: 30 minutes
+ overnight marinating
Cooking time: 15 minutes
Makes 10 skewers

1/4 onion, chopped
2 cloves garlic, crushed
1 tablespoon grated fresh ginger
2 tablespoons lemon juice
1 teaspoon grated lemon rind
3 teaspoons ground coriander
3 teaspoons ground cumin
3 teaspoons garam masala
1/3 cup (90 g/3 oz) plain yoghurt
1 teaspoon salt
750 g (1 1/2 lb) chicken thigh fillets, cut into cubes

1 Soak 10 wooden skewers in water for about 30 minutes to prevent them burning while cooking.
2 In a food processor, finely chop the onion, garlic, ginger, lemon juice and rind, coriander, cumin and garam masala. Stir in the yoghurt and salt.
3 Thread 4–5 chicken cubes onto each skewer and place in a large shallow dish. Coat the skewers with the spice mixture. Marinate for several hours or overnight, covered, in the refrigerator.
4 Cook the skewers in batches on a barbecue or chargrill pan, or under a hot grill, for 3–4 minutes on each side, until golden brown and cooked.

NUTRITION PER SKEWER
Protein 15 g; Fat 4 g; Carbohydrate 1 g; Dietary Fibre 0 g; Cholesterol 55 mg; 420 kJ (100 cal)

Soak the skewers in water so that they do not burn during cooking.

Finely chop the onion, garlic, lemon juice and rind, and spices in a food processor.

Take the skewers and thread 4–5 pieces of chicken onto each one.

Cook the skewers for 3–4 minutes on each side, until golden brown.

RED CURRY PRAWNS WITH FRAGRANT RICE

Preparation time: 25–30 minutes
Total cooking time: 35 minutes
Serves 2–3

Fragrant Rice
1½ cups (375 ml/12 fl oz) water
1 cup (200 g/6½ oz) fragrant jasmine rice

½ cup (125 ml/4 fl oz) coconut cream
2 spring onions, finely chopped
2 stems lemon grass, white part only, finely chopped
2 tablespoons red curry paste
3 kaffir lime leaves, shredded
2½ cups (600 ml/20 fl oz) coconut milk
2 kaffir lime leaves, extra, slightly crushed
1 kg (2 lb) large raw prawns, peeled and deveined
2 tablespoons fish sauce
1 tablespoon grated palm sugar
¼ cup (15 g/½ oz) fresh small basil leaves
2 kaffir lime leaves, shredded, to garnish
2 small red chillies, seeded and cut into fine lengthways strips, to garnish

1 To make Fragrant Rice: Place the water in a heavy-based pan and bring to the boil. Slowly add the rice and a good pinch of salt. Stir once and return to the boil. Cover and reduce the heat to very low. Cook for 18 minutes, then remove the lid and allow the steam to escape for 5 minutes. Stir gently with a fork to fluff up the grains.

2 While the rice is cooking, heat the coconut cream in a large pan. Add the spring onion, lemon grass, curry paste and shredded kaffir lime leaves. Cook, stirring, for 4–5 minutes, until fragrant.

3 Add the coconut milk and crushed kaffir lime leaves to the pan; bring to the boil and add the prawns. Reduce the heat and simmer for 10 minutes, or until the prawns are cooked.

4 Season to taste with fish sauce and palm sugar (use up to the suggested amount). Stir through the basil leaves. Serve the prawns spooned over the fragrant rice, garnished with lime leaves and chillies.

NUTRITION PER SERVE (3)
Protein 80 g; Fat 55 g; Carbohydrate 70 g; Dietary Fibre 3 g; Cholesterol 495 mg; 4635 kJ (1100 cal)

Coarsely grate up to 1 tablespoon of palm sugar (according to taste) for seasoning.

Gently fluff the grains of cooked rice with a fork.

Add the spring onion, lemon grass, red curry paste and kaffir lime leaves.

MALAY LAMB CURRY

Preparation time: 30 minutes
Total cooking time: 2 hours 15 minutes
Serves 4

1 tablespoon oil
1 kg (2 lb) lamb best neck chops, trimmed
1 onion, chopped
1 tablespoon grated fresh ginger
4 cloves garlic, crushed
2 teaspoons ground cumin
2 teaspoons ground coriander
1 teaspoon ground turmeric
1 tablespoon curry powder
1 tablespoon seeded and finely sliced green chilli
2 tomatoes, chopped
2½ cups (600 ml/20 fl oz) chicken stock
4 potatoes, cut into large chunks
1 tablespoon fresh coriander leaves

1 Heat the oil and brown the lamb in batches over high heat; transfer to a plate. Add the onion to the pan, reduce the heat and cook until soft and transparent. Stir in the ginger, garlic, cumin, coriander, turmeric, curry powder and chilli. Cook, stirring, for 1 minute, until fragrant.

2 Return the lamb to the pan and combine well with the spice mixture. Add the tomato and stock. Bring to the boil, reduce the heat to very low and simmer, covered, for 1½ hours.

3 Add the potato to the pan and cook, uncovered, for 30 minutes, stirring occasionally, until the liquid is a thick, rich sauce. Season to taste with salt and black pepper. Serve scattered with fresh coriander leaves and accompanied by steamed rice.

NUTRITION PER SERVE
Protein 55 g; Fat 20 g; Carbohydrate 20 g; Dietary Fibre 5 g; Cholesterol 165 mg; 2060 kJ (490 cal)

Stir in the ginger, garlic, spices and chilli until fragrant.

Add the chopped tomatoes and chicken stock to the lamb.

Add the potatoes to the pan and cook, uncovered, for 30 minutes.

SMOKED FISH KEDGEREE

Preparation time: 20 minutes
Total cooking time: 30 minutes
Serves 4

600 g (1¼ lb) smoked haddock
50 g (1⅔ oz) butter
1 onion, finely chopped
2 teaspoons curry powder
1 teaspoon ground cumin
1 teaspoon ground coriander
2 teaspoons seeded and finely sliced green chilli
1 cup (200 g/6½ oz) basmati rice
2¾ cups (660 ml/22 fl oz) chicken or fish stock
1 cinnamon stick
⅓ cup (80 ml/2¾ fl oz) cream
2 hard-boiled eggs, finely chopped
2 tablespoons finely chopped fresh parsley
2 tablespoons finely chopped fresh coriander

1 Place the haddock in batches in a large shallow pan, skin-side up. Cover with boiling water and simmer very gently for about 10 minutes. The fish is cooked when the flesh flakes easily when tested with a fork. Drain and pat dry with paper towels. Remove the skin and bones and flake into bite-size chunks.

2 Heat the butter in a large saucepan and add the onion. Cook until soft and golden, then add the curry powder, cumin, coriander and chilli. Cook, stirring, for 1 minute. Add the rice, stir well, then pour in the stock and add the cinnamon stick. Cover with a tightly fitting lid and simmer over a gentle heat for about 12 minutes, or until the rice is tender.

3 Remove the cinnamon stick and gently stir in the flaked haddock. Fold through the cream, chopped egg and the herbs. Season to taste with salt and freshly ground black pepper and serve immediately.

NUTRITION PER SERVE
Protein 45 g; Fat 25 g; Carbohydrate 45 g; Dietary Fibre 2 g; Cholesterol 255 mg; 2355 kJ (560 cal)

When the fish is cooked, the flesh will flake easily when tested with a fork.

Add the rice to the onion, curry powder, cumin, coriander and chilli and stir well.

Fold through the cream, chopped egg, parsley and coriander.

CHICKEN WITH CREAMY CURRY SAUCE

Preparation time: 25 minutes
Total cooking time: 40 minutes
Serves 4

1 tablespoon oil
50 g (1 2/3 oz) butter
1 onion, chopped
2 cloves garlic, crushed
2 teaspoons grated fresh ginger
1 green chilli, seeded and finely chopped
1/4 teaspoon crushed cardamom seeds
1 teaspoon garam masala
1 teaspoon ground turmeric
1 tablespoon plain flour
1 1/2 cups (375 ml/12 fl oz) chicken stock
1/3 cup (80 ml/2 3/4 fl oz) brandy
1/2 cup (125 ml/4 fl oz) cream
4 large chicken breast fillets, each cut into thirds and flattened with a meat mallet
flaked toasted almonds and chopped fresh coriander, to serve

1 Heat the oil and half the butter in a large, deep frying pan. Add the onion and cook over medium heat until soft and transparent. Add the garlic, ginger and chilli and cook for 1 minute, then add the cardamom, garam masala and turmeric and cook for 1 minute. Stir in the flour and cook for a minute.

2 Remove from the heat. Mix in gradually the combined chicken stock, brandy and cream, stirring constantly. Return to the heat. Cook, stirring, until the sauce boils and thickens. Cover; simmer over low heat for 15 minutes.

3 Meanwhile, heat the remaining butter in a frying pan and brown the chicken pieces. Add the chicken to the sauce and cook for a further 10–15 minutes to reduce. Season with salt and black pepper. Serve scattered with toasted almonds and coriander.

NUTRITION PER SERVE
Protein 40 g; Fat 35 g; Carbohydrate 5 g; Dietary Fibre 2 g; Cholesterol 155 mg; 2295 kJ (545 cal)

Seed and finely chop 1 fresh green chilli with a sharp knife.

Cook the onion over a moderate heat until it turns soft and transparent.

Gradually add the combined stock, brandy and cream, stirring constantly.

RED LENTIL CURRY

Preparation time: 15 minutes
Total cooking time: 30 minutes
Serves 4

1 cup (250 g/8 oz) red lentils, rinsed and drained
2 cups (500 ml/16 fl oz) vegetable stock
1/2 teaspoon ground turmeric
50 g (1 2/3 oz) ghee
1 onion, chopped
2 cloves garlic, finely chopped
1 large green chilli, seeded and finely chopped
2 teaspoons ground cumin
2 teaspoons ground coriander
2 tomatoes, chopped
1/2 cup (125 ml/4 fl oz) coconut milk

1 Place the lentils, stock and turmeric in a large heavy-based pan. Bring to the boil, reduce the heat and simmer, covered, for 10 minutes, or until just tender. Stir occasionally and check the mixture is not catching on the bottom of the pan.

2 Meanwhile, heat the ghee in a small frying pan and add the onion. Cook until soft and golden and add the garlic, chilli, cumin and coriander. Cook, stirring, for 2–3 minutes until fragrant. Stir the onions and spices into the lentil mixture and then add the tomato. Simmer over very low heat for 5 minutes, stirring frequently.

3 Season to taste with salt and pepper, and stir in the coconut milk until heated through. Serve with naan bread or rice.

NUTRITION PER SERVE
Protein 15 g; Fat 20 g; Carbohydrate 25 g; Dietary Fibre 10 g; Cholesterol 35 mg; 1500 kJ (355 cal)

Stir the lentil mixture occasionally so that it does not stick to the bottom of the pan.

Add the chopped tomato and simmer for 5 minutes, stirring frequently.

Stir through the coconut milk until it has combined with the mixture.

Remove the seeds and white membrane from the chilli with a knife.

Cook the spices in a frying pan until the seeds pop and blacken.

Return the lamb to the pan, add the stock and cook for another 1 1/4 hours.

Add the spinach and continue cooking until it has just wilted.

LAMB SAAG

Preparation time: 25 minutes
Total cooking time: 1 hour 40 minutes
Serves 4

1 long green chilli
3 cloves garlic, chopped
2 cm (3/4 inch) piece fresh ginger, grated
3 tablespoons oil
1 kg (2 lb) boneless lean lamb (leg or shoulder), cut into cubes
1 teaspoon fenugreek seeds
1/2 teaspoon cumin seeds
1 teaspoon black mustard seeds
1 cinnamon stick
6 cardamom pods
2 onions, chopped
2 teaspoons ground turmeric
1 teaspoon ground cumin
1 teaspoon chilli powder
1 teaspoon ground coriander
2 bay leaves
1 cup (250 ml/8 fl oz) beef stock
900 g (1 lb 13 1/3 oz) English spinach, finely shredded
1/2 teaspoon salt
1 tablespoon chopped fresh coriander
1/3 cup (90 g/3 oz) plain yoghurt

1 Remove the seeds and white membrane from the chilli, and finely chop. Set aside with the garlic and ginger. Heat 2 tablespoons of oil in a large frying pan and brown the lamb in batches. Drain on paper towels.
2 Combine the fenugreek, cumin, mustard, cinnamon and cardamom in a frying pan. Cook, for 1 minute, stirring constantly, until the seeds pop and blacken. Set aside. Heat the remaining oil in a pan; add the onion. Cook for 3–4 minutes over medium heat, then stir in the roasted spices.
3 Add the garlic mixture, turmeric, cumin, chilli powder, coriander and bay leaves to the onion. Cook, for 1 minute, stirring constantly. Return the lamb to the pan, add the stock and reduce the heat to low. Cook, covered, for 1 1/4 hours, stirring occasionally.
4 Add the spinach and salt. Cover and cook for 5 minutes, or until just wilted. Stir in the coriander and yoghurt, discard the cinnamon stick and bay leaves and serve.

NUTRITION PER SERVE
Protein 65 g; Fat 25 g; Carbohydrate 5 g; Dietary Fibre 10 g; Cholesterol 170 mg; 2100 kJ (500 cal)

BUTTER CHICKEN

Preparation time: 30 minutes
+ 4 hours marinating
Total cooking time: 20 minutes
Serves 4

1 kg (2 lb) chicken thigh fillets
1 teaspoon salt
1/4 cup (60 ml/2 fl oz) lemon juice
1 cup (250 g/8 oz) yoghurt
1 onion, chopped
2 cloves garlic, crushed
3 cm (1 1/4 inch) piece fresh ginger, grated
1 green chilli, chopped
3 teaspoons garam masala
2 teaspoons yellow food colouring
1 teaspoon red food colouring
1/2 cup tomato purée
1/2 cup (125 ml/4 fl oz) water
2 cm (3/4 inch) piece fresh ginger, extra, finely grated
1 cup (250 ml/8 fl oz) cream
2 teaspoons sugar
1/4 teaspoon chilli powder
1 tablespoon lemon juice, extra
1 teaspoon ground cumin
100 g (3 1/3 oz) butter

1 Cut the chicken into 2 cm (3/4 inch) thick strips. Sprinkle with the salt and lemon juice.
2 Place the yoghurt, onion, garlic, ginger, chilli and 2 teaspoons of the garam masala in a food processor and blend until smooth.
3 Combine the food colourings in a small bowl. Brush over the chicken and turn the strips to coat the meat all over. Add the yoghurt mixture and toss to combine. Cover and refrigerate for 4 hours. Remove the chicken from the marinade and allow to drain for 5 minutes.
4 Preheat the oven to hot 220°C (425°F/Gas 7). Place the chicken in a shallow baking dish and bake for 15 minutes, or until it is tender. Drain off any excess juice, cover loosely with foil and keep warm.
5 Mix together the tomato purée and water in a large jug. Add the ginger, cream, remaining teaspoon of garam marsala, sugar, chilli powder, lemon juice and cumin, and stir to thoroughly combine.
6 Melt the butter in a large pan over medium heat. Stir in the tomato mixture and bring to the boil. Cook for 2 minutes, then reduce the heat and add the chicken pieces. Stir to coat the chicken with the sauce and simmer for a further 2 minutes or until completely heated through. Serve with rice and garnish with some shredded kaffir lime leaves.

NUTRITION PER SERVE
Protein 55 g; Fat 60 g; Carbohydrate 10 g; Dietary Fibre 2 g; Cholesterol 330 mg; 3390 kJ (805 cal)

COOK'S FILE

Note: The chicken can also be marinated overnight in the refrigerator. It is important to always use a non-metallic dish when marinating.
Hint: Kaffir lime leaves are available from most supermarkets, Asian food stores and good fruit and vegetable shops.
Variation: Chicken pieces can be substituted for the chicken thigh fillets. Score the thickest part of the meat with a knife and then bake for 30–40 minutes, or until tender.

Sprinkle the salt and lemon juice over the strips of chicken.

Process the yoghurt, onion, garlic, ginger, chilli and garam masala.

Brush the food colourings over the chicken, coating the meat thoroughly.

Drain any excess juice from the baked chicken pieces.

Add the ginger, cream, garam masala, sugar, chilli, lemon juice and cumin.

Add the chicken pieces to the pan and stir to coat with the sauce.

THAI FISH AND NOODLE CURRY SOUP

Preparation time: 25–30 minutes
Total cooking time: 20 minutes
Serves 4

Sauce
4 spring onions, chopped
2 cloves garlic, chopped
2 slices galangal, roughly chopped
1 stem lemon grass, finely sliced
2 teaspoons chopped fresh ginger
3 dried chillies, seeds removed
1/2 teaspoon salt
1 teaspoon shrimp paste

1 cup (250 ml/8 fl oz) vegetable stock
2 cups (500 ml/16 fl oz) coconut milk
300 g (9 2/3 oz) white fish fillets, cut into cubes
1/2 cup (125 ml/4 fl oz) coconut cream
2 tablespoons fish sauce
400 g (12 2/3 oz) cooked fresh rice spaghetti noodles

Accompaniments
1 cup (90 g/3 oz) bean sprouts
1 small Lebanese cucumber, finely sliced
1 cup (50 g/1 2/3 oz) fresh basil leaves, shredded
1 cup (45 g/1 1/2 oz) finely sliced Chinese cabbage
2 teaspoons dried chilli flakes

1 To make Sauce: Simmer all sauce ingredients in a small pan with 1 cup (250 ml/8 fl oz) water over low heat for about 10 minutes. Remove from the heat; cool slightly. Blend in a food processor or blender.

2 Place the Sauce in a large pan; add the stock and coconut milk. Bring to the boil and reduce the heat. Add the fish and simmer, stirring regularly, to prevent sticking, for 5–6 minutes, or until the fish is cooked.

3 Stir in the coconut cream and fish sauce until just heated through. Arrange a portion of the noodles and a little of each of the Accompaniments in individual bowls. Spoon the Sauce over the noodles just before serving.

NUTRITION PER SERVE
Protein 25 g; Fat 35 g; Carbohydrate 30 g; Dietary Fibre 3 g; Cholesterol 55 mg; 2185 kJ (520 cal)

Simmer the Sauce ingredients in a small pan with 1 cup (250 ml/8 fl oz) of water.

Add the cubed fish to the pan and simmer for 5–6 minutes.

Add the coconut cream to the pan before seasoning with the fish sauce.

Cook the chicken fillets until tender and browned on both sides.

Fry the curry powder in a dry frying pan until fragrant.

Carefully cut the orange into segments between the membrane.

Whisk the Curry Dressing well before drizzling over the salad.

CHICKEN AND CITRUS SALAD WITH CURRY DRESSING

Preparation time: 20 minutes
Total cooking time: 15 minutes
Serves 4

4 chicken breast fillets
1 tablespoon olive oil
2 oranges
1 lettuce
250 g (8 oz) watercress
15 g (1/2 oz) chives

Curry Dressing
3 teaspoons curry powder
2 spring onions, finely sliced
2 tablespoons olive oil
2 tablespoons sunflower oil
1 tablespoon balsamic vinegar
2 teaspoons soft brown sugar
1 teaspoon chopped green chilli

1 Trim the chicken fillets of any fat and sinew. Heat the oil in a frying pan; cook the chicken over moderate heat for about 7 minutes on each side, until browned and tender. Allow to cool and cut across the grain into thick strips.

2 To make Curry Dressing: Dry-fry the curry powder in a frying pan for 1 minute, until fragrant. Cool slightly, then place in a small bowl with the remaining ingredients and whisk to combine. Season to taste with salt and black pepper. Set aside to allow the flavours to develop.

3 Peel the oranges, removing all the white pith. Cut into segments, between the membrane; discard any pips.

4 Wash and dry the lettuce leaves and watercress and arrange on a large platter. Place the chicken pieces and orange segments on top. Whisk the dressing again; drizzle over the salad. Chop the chives into short lengths and scatter over the top.

NUTRITION PER SERVE
Protein 25 g; Fat 25 g; Carbohydrate 10 g; Dietary Fibre 2 g; Cholesterol 55 mg; 1590 kJ (380 cal)

FRAGRANT COCONUT BEEF

Preparation time: 30 minutes
Total cooking time: 1 hour 40 minutes
Serves 4

Spice Paste
6 dried chillies
2 spring onions, chopped
2 cm (3/4 inch) galangal, chopped
2 stems lemon grass, white part only, sliced
2 cloves garlic, chopped
1 teaspoon grated fresh ginger

2 tablespoons vegetable oil
1 cinnamon stick, broken
2 cloves
4 star anise
2 cardamom pods, bruised
1 kg (2 lb) chuck steak, cubed
2 cups (500 ml/16 fl oz) coconut milk
1 tablespoon tamarind concentrate
3 kaffir lime leaves, shredded
4 fresh curry leaves
1 cup (55 g/1 3/4 oz) flaked coconut
1 teaspoon sugar

1 To make Spice Paste: Soak the chillies in boiling water for 10 minutes to soften them. Drain and finely chop in a food processor with all the other Spice Paste ingredients.

2 Heat the oil in a wok or a large frying pan. Add the Spice Paste and the whole spices and stir-fry over medium heat for 5 minutes. Add the chuck steak cubes, in batches if necessary, and cook over high heat, stirring constantly, for 6–8 minutes, or until the steak has browned.

3 Stir in the coconut milk and tamarind concentrate. Reduce the heat to very low and simmer for 30 minutes, stirring occasionally. Add the kaffir lime and curry leaves, coconut, sugar and season with salt. Simmer for 1 hour, or until the meat is tender and the liquid has dried up. Discard the whole spices and curry leaves before serving.

NUTRITION PER SERVE
Protein 55 g; Fat 55 g; Carbohydrate 7 g; Dietary Fibre 4 g; Cholesterol 170 mg; 3060 kJ (730 cal)

Soften the chillies by soaking them in boiling water for 10 minutes.

Add the Spice Paste and whole spices to the oil in the wok or frying pan.

Stir in the coconut milk and tamarind, reduce the heat and simmer.

SPICY PUMPKIN PUFFS

Preparation time: 20 minutes
Total cooking time: 45–50 minutes
Makes 20

1 tablespoon vegetable oil
1 onion, finely chopped
3 fresh curry leaves
1 tablespoon brown mustard seeds
2 teaspoons mild Madras curry powder
1/2 teaspoon chilli powder
1/2 teaspoon ground turmeric
350 g (11 1/4 oz) pumpkin, peeled and diced
1/2 cup (80 g/2 2/3 oz) frozen peas
3/4 cup (185 ml/6 fl oz) chicken stock
5 sheets ready-rolled puff pastry
1 egg, lightly beaten

1 Heat the oil in a frying pan and sauté the onion for 2–3 minutes over moderate heat. Add the curry leaves and mustard seeds and fry for 1–2 minutes, or until mustard seeds pop. Add the curry powder, chilli powder and turmeric and fry for 30 seconds.

2 Add the pumpkin to the pan and stir for 1–2 minutes, or until well coated with spices. Add the peas and stock to the pan, stir gently and simmer for 8–10 minutes, or until the pumpkin is tender and most of the liquid has evaporated. Remove from the heat and cool completely.

3 Preheat the oven to hot 220°C (425°F/Gas 7). Brush two oven trays lightly with oil. Cut 10 cm (4 inch) circles from the pastry sheets, and spoon 1 tablespoon of the mixture onto the centre of each. Brush the edges with beaten egg and fold over to enclose the filling. Roll and fold the edges to seal. Place the puffs on the trays and brush with the remaining beaten egg. Bake for 25–30 minutes, until puffed and golden.

NUTRITION PER PUFF
Protein 4 g; Fat 10 g; Carbohydrate 15 g; Dietary Fibre 1 g; Cholesterol 20 mg; 760 kJ (180 cal)

Add the curry leaves and mustard seeds to the onion and fry for 1–2 minutes.

Gently insert a knife into the pumpkin to check if it is tender.

Brush along the edge of each pastry circle with beaten egg.

Curry Essentials

Knowing what combination of herbs and spices to add to a particular curry dish can sometimes seem daunting. The following guide, with its descriptions and suggested uses, will help you appreciate the different flavours, and make cooking a more enjoyable and creative experience.

Basil
There are many varieties of this herb from the Mediterranean and from Southeast Asia. All have a strong aroma and flavour.
Asian Sweet (Bai Horapha) is similar to European Sweet basil. It has a sweet anise flavour and is used in red and green curries as an aromatic or to garnish salads and soups.
European Sweet has large green leaves and a strong aroma when chopped or ground. Use as a substitute when Asian basils are unobtainable.
Holy Basil has a pungent, clove-like taste. The narrow leaves, tinged a purple-red, are added during cooking.
Lemon Basil (Bai Manglaek) has small lemon-scented leaves, which are added to fish and seafood dishes to mask the 'fishy' odours.

Cardamom
The whole pods and seeds are used in Indian-style curries. The green pods are bruised with the back of a knife to release the flavour and should be removed from the dish before serving. The roasted black seeds are crushed or ground for garam masala and dry powder blends.

Cinnamon
This dry, flaky bark of a Sri Lankan tree is available as a stick or as ground powder. It is used to flavour curries. Always remove cinnamon sticks before serving.

Coconut milk and cream
This is the liquid extracted from the fresh coconut flesh. The first extract produces the rich, thick coconut cream, which is added sparingly, usually at the end of cooking, over low heat.

Coconut milk is the subsequent extractions of the coconut flesh. It has a thinner consistency, and is used in Thai and Malaysian style curries.

Block coconut cream can also be used when only small quantities are required. Blend equal quantities of the block with hot water until it reaches a smooth consistency. Coconut milk powder, available in packets in supermarkets, has a long storage life and can be diluted to either coconut cream or coconut milk, by following the instructions on the packet.

Coriander
Also known as cilantro or Chinese parsley, coriander is commonly used in curry dishes. The seeds are dry-fried, ground and usually added at the beginning of Indian curries. The stems and roots are used in fresh curry pastes, especially Thai. The

leaves are added at the end of cooking, or as a garnish to retain their fresh, peppery flavour and bright green colour.

Cumin
These pungent yellow-brown seeds are roasted whole then ground or finely crushed in a spice mill or mortar and pestle. Cumin is a key ingredient in Indian style curries.

Curry leaves
Available fresh or dried, curry leaves are used whole in cooking. They impart a mild curry flavour and are removed before serving.

Fenugreek
This is a pungent and sometimes bitter spice, which should be used sparingly. It is an essential component of commercial curry powders. The seeds are very hard, but can be ground in a mortar and pestle.

Fish sauce
A thin, clear, brown sauce used extensively in Thai and Vietnamese cooking. It is made from fermented prawns or small fish and imparts a salty, subtle fish flavour.

Galangal
A member of the ginger family, galangal is similar in appearance to ginger but has pink markings and shoots. It has a distinctive peppery taste and is used to flavour Asian curry pastes, stir fries and soups. The spicy flavour intensifies with age and the flesh changes colour to yellow. Take care when handling, as the juice will stain clothes and hands. If fresh is not available, use dried galangal (from Asian groceries), but leave it to soak in hot water for 20 minutes before you start cooking.

Ginger
This fresh root is readily available and widely used in curry dishes. Look for root pieces with a smooth, shiny skin and a fresh, aromatic odour. Scrape the skin gently from the flesh before starting to chop or grate.

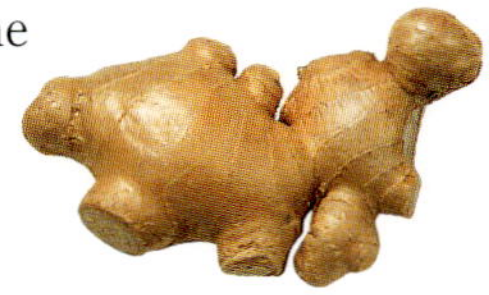

Kaffir lime and leaves
This Southeast Asian lime has a distinctive knobbly, dark green skin and a strong citrus fragrance. The shredded or finely grated rind adds freshness to curry pastes and chilli dishes. The glossy, green leaves are added whole to curries and removed before serving. Kaffir lime leaves are available fresh or dried from supermarkets, greengrocers or Asian food stores. Standard lime rind and young leaves can be used as a substitute, if necessary.

Lemon grass
A long, aromatic stemmy herb, lemon grass is very popular in Thai cooking. Only the white bottom section of the stem is used. To release the fresh citrus flavour, remove the tough, outer layers, bruise the stem with the back of a knife, and finely slice or chop. The whole stem may be used in curries and removed before serving. Dried lemon grass is available, although inferior in flavour. Soak in boiling water for half an hour before use.

Mustard seeds
A common ingredient in curries, mustard seeds are fried before grinding to release the essential oils and increase the flavour. Black and brown mustard seeds are the smallest and the hottest, whereas white mustard seeds are the largest and the most mild.

Palm sugar
Popular in Southeast Asian and Indian dishes, this sugar is made from the sap of various species of palm tree. It is a pale golden or dark brown colour with a coarse grain and is usually grated before use. Substitute with soft brown or demerara sugar.

Saffron threads
These reddish-orange threads are the stigmas of a crocus flower. Saffron is the most expensive spice in the world, but only a small amount is needed to give a vivid colour and subtle flavour. Infuse in a small quantity of hot milk or water for 15 minutes or toast the threads in a dry pan and crush them before adding to curries or rice.

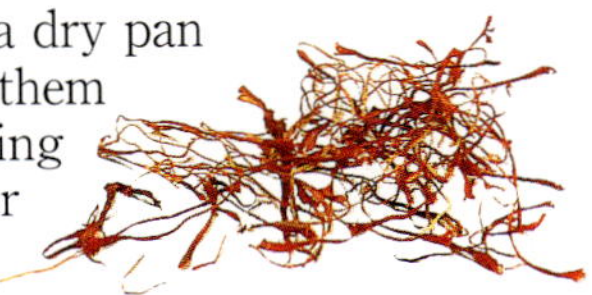

Shrimp paste
This pungent brown paste is made by salting, fermenting and grinding shrimps. Use sparingly to flavour curry pastes or sauces. It is available in a block or thick paste from Asian food stores.

Star anise
A dark brown, star-shaped pod with a distinctive aniseed flavour. Star anise is used whole to flavour curries. Make sure you remove the pods before serving.

Tamarind concentrate
A sour liquid made from the fruits of the tamarind tree, this is used to give tartness to curries and Indian dishes. It is also available as a pulp, which must be soaked in hot water for 5 minutes and then strained before use.

Turmeric
Turmeric is a key ingredient of curry powder, giving it a bitter flavour and distinctive bright yellow-orange colour. Widely available as a powder, this rhizome can also be purchased fresh from speciality greengrocers or Asian food stores. Peel or gently scrape away the skin of the fresh root and slice or grate.

CURRIED LENTIL SOUP

Preparation time: 15 minutes
Total cooking time: 1 hour
Serves 4

50 g ($1\frac{2}{3}$ oz) ghee or butter
1 large onion, chopped
2 cloves garlic, finely chopped
2 tablespoons Madras (hot) curry powder
1 teaspoon black mustard seeds
300 g ($9\frac{2}{3}$ oz) potatoes, diced
220 g (7 oz) dried red lentils
4 cups (1 litre) chicken stock
$\frac{1}{2}$ teaspoon salt
2 tablespoons lemon juice
thick plain yoghurt, to serve
2 tablespoons finely chopped fresh coriander, to garnish

1 Heat the ghee in a heavy-based pan. Cook the onion and garlic for 3 minutes, or until just softened. Add the curry powder and mustard seeds and cook for 2 minutes, stirring well.

2 Add the potato and cook for 6–7 minutes, stirring regularly, until the potato is golden brown and just tender. Add the lentils, stock and salt. Bring to the boil, reduce the heat and simmer for 45 minutes, skimming off any foam from the top of the soup while cooking, until the potato is soft and the soup is thick. Add extra water if the soup becomes too thick.

3 Add the lemon juice and season with plenty of salt and pepper. Serve topped with yoghurt and sprinkled with coriander.

NUTRITION PER SERVE
Protein 20 g; Fat 15 g; Carbohydrate 35 g; Dietary Fibre 10 g; Cholesterol 35 mg; 1460 kJ (345 cal)

Add the curry powder and mustard seeds to the pan.

During cooking, skim any foam from the top of the soup.

Season the soup to taste with plenty of salt and pepper.

BEEF VINDALOO

Preparation time: 20 minutes
Total cooking time: 1 hour 45 minutes
Serves 4

1 kg (2 lb) chuck, blade or skirt steak
2 tablespoons ghee or oil
3 onions, sliced
1/2 teaspoon ground cumin
1 tablespoon ground coriander
1/2 teaspoon ground cardamom
1 teaspoon ground fenugreek
1 teaspoon chilli powder
1 teaspoon ground turmeric
1 teaspoon mustard powder
1 cinnamon stick
3 teaspoons grated fresh ginger
3 cloves garlic, crushed
1/3 cup (80ml/2 3/4 fl oz) brown vinegar
1/2 cup (125 ml/4 fl oz) beef stock
1 teaspoon sugar

1 Cut the steak into bite-size cubes. Heat the ghee or oil in a large pan and brown the meat in two batches. Transfer to a plate.

2 Add the onion to the pan; cook over medium heat for 5 minutes, or until very soft and lightly golden. Add the spices, ginger and garlic and cook, stirring, for 1 more minute. Return the meat to the pan and stir until well coated in the spices.

3 Add the vinegar, stock, sugar, and season with salt and pepper to taste. Bring just to the boil, reduce the heat to low and simmer, covered, for about 1 1/2 hours, or until the meat is very tender. Discard the cinnamon stick. Serve with plain or basmati rice. Garnish with a little finely grated fresh ginger.

NUTRITION PER SERVE
Protein 55 g; Fat 15 g; Carbohydrate 5 g; Dietary Fibre 1 g; Cholesterol 190 mg; 1600 kJ (380 cal)

Cook the meat in batches—if the pan is overcrowded it will stew in its own juices.

Add the spices, ginger and garlic to the pan and cook for 1 minute.

Add the remaining ingredients to the pan and bring to the boil.

CHICKEN BIRYANI

Preparation time: 1 hour 30 minutes plus 3–4 hours marinating
Total cooking time: about 2 hours
Serves 6

Marinade
6 cardamom pods
3 onions, peeled
3 cloves garlic
5 cm (2 inch) piece fresh ginger, sliced
8 cloves or $\frac{1}{4}$ teaspoon ground cloves
1 teaspoon whole black peppercorns
1 teaspoon ground cumin
1 teaspoon ground cinnamon
$1\frac{1}{2}$ tablespoons black poppy seeds
$\frac{1}{4}$ teaspoon ground nutmeg
1 teaspoon salt
2 tablespoons lemon juice
250 g (8 oz) natural yoghurt

1 kg (2 lb) chicken pieces, cut into small pieces
$\frac{1}{3}$ cup (80 ml/$2\frac{3}{4}$ fl oz) oil
3 bay leaves
2 whole cardamom pods, lightly crushed
3 onions, very finely sliced
2 tablespoons raisins
$1\frac{1}{2}$ cups (300g/$9\frac{2}{3}$ oz) long-grain white rice
$\frac{1}{4}$ cup (60 ml/2 fl oz) milk
1 teaspoon sugar
1 teaspoon saffron threads
plain yoghurt, to serve
3 tablespoons toasted cashews, to garnish

1 To make Marinade: Crush the cardamom pods with the flat side of a large knife blade to release the seeds; discard the pods. Chop the onions, garlic and ginger in a food processor. Add the cardamom seeds, cloves, peppercorns, cumin, cinnamon, poppy seeds, nutmeg, salt and lemon juice and process to a smooth paste. Stir in the yoghurt and set aside.

2 Prick the skin of the chicken with a fork (this helps the flavour infuse into the chicken) and place in a large mixing bowl. Add the marinade and mix well to thoroughly coat the chicken, then refrigerate for 3–4 hours, or overnight.

3 Heat about 3 tablespoons of the oil in a heavy-based frying pan over low heat. Add the bay leaves and whole cardamom pods and toss in the oil. Cook for 2 minutes, being careful not to burn. Remove the bay leaves and set aside; discard the cardamom pods. Add the onion and fry over low heat for 8 minutes, or until a rich golden colour. Remove with a slotted spoon leaving the oil in the pan. Drain on paper towels. Quickly fry the raisins until plump; set aside with the onions Reserve the remaining oil.

4 Place the chicken and the marinade in a heavy-based flameproof casserole dish; bring slowly to the boil. Cover and simmer for 15 minutes. Using tongs or a slotted spoon, remove the chicken, leaving as much marinade in the pan as possible. Reduce the marinade down, cooking it over a low heat until only about 1 cup (250 ml/8 fl oz) remains. Return the chicken to the pan and toss to coat in the thickened sauce. Cover and set aside while preparing the rice.

5 Add the rice to a large pan of boiling water and cook for 7 minutes. (Do not cook the rice until tender.) Drain the rice into a colander. Meanwhile heat the milk and sugar, pour into a bowl, add the saffron and soak for 5 minutes.

6 Preheat the oven to slow 150°C (300°F/Gas 2). Spoon the rice over the spice-coated chicken and pour over the the saffron mixture. Streak the

Crush the cardamom pods to release the seeds with the flat side of a knife.

Prick the skin of the chicken with a fork to help the flavour infuse into the meat.

Remove the onions with a slotted spoon, keeping as much oil as possible in the pan.

orange colour gently through the rice with a fork. Pour over the reserved flavoured oil, and scatter with bay leaves. Cover the dish tightly with foil. Bake for 1 hour, until the rice and chicken are tender. Serve topped with the onions, raisins and yoghurt, and garnished with cashews.

NUTRITION PER SERVE
Protein 40 g; Fat 45 g; Carbohydrate 60 g; Dietary Fibre 4 g; Cholesterol 140 mg; 3305 kJ (785 cal)

COOK'S FILE

Note: Biryani is a very regal and special dish which is usually served at elaborate weddings. It is definitely worth all the effort to cook, so do not cut corners.

Cook the marinade over low heat until reduced and thickened.

Add the saffron threads to the heated milk and sugar mixture.

Gently streak the saffron mixture through the rice using a fork.

POPPY SEED LAMB KEBABS

Preparation time: 30 minutes
+ 1 hour marinating
Total cooking time: about 10 minutes
Serves 4

1 large onion, finely chopped
2 cloves garlic, finely chopped
1 heaped teaspoon poppy seeds
1 teaspoon ground coriander
1 teaspoon ground cumin
1 teaspoon ground turmeric
1/2 teaspoon ground fenugreek
4 tablespoons plain yoghurt
500 g (1 lb) diced lamb
50 g (1 2/3 oz) ghee, melted

1 Pound the onion in a mortar and pestle with 2 tablespoons water until quite smooth, or use a small food processor. Squeeze the onion through a clean piece of muslin or chux (kitchen cloth) to extract 2 tablespoons of onion juice. Discard the pulp and extra juice. Combine the juice, garlic, poppy seeds, all the spices, yoghurt and lamb, mixing well. Cover and refrigerate for 1 hour or marinate overnight for a fuller flavour.

2 Soak 12 small wooden skewers in water for 20 minutes; drain. Thread 3–4 pieces of lamb onto each skewer.

3 Line a grill plate with foil. Cook the kebabs under medium-high heat, basting regularly with the ghee, for about 7 minutes, turning often. Serve with a crisp salad, tangy chutney such as mango and lime, and steamed rice.

NUTRITION PER SERVE
Protein 30 g; Fat 20 g; Carbohydrate 3 g; Dietary Fibre 1 g; Cholesterol 120 mg; 1230 kJ (290 cal)

Squeeze the onion through a clean piece of muslin or chux to extract the juice.

Thread 3–4 pieces of lamb onto the middle of each skewer.

Baste the kebabs regularly with the ghee while cooking.

Brush the chicken with lemon juice and marinate for 30 minutes.

Process the tandoori mixture until it becomes smooth and pinkish in colour.

Thoroughly coat the chicken pieces with the yoghurt mixture.

Place the chicken on a wire rack over a large baking dish.

TANDOORI CHICKEN

Preparation time: 30 minutes
+ 4 hours 30 minutes refrigeration
Total cooking time: 45 minutes
Serves 4–6

6 chicken thigh fillets
1/4 cup (60 ml/2 fl oz) lemon juice
3 teaspoons ground coriander
1 tablespoon ground cumin
1/2 small onion, chopped
4 cloves garlic
1 tablespoon grated fresh ginger
1 tablespoon lemon juice, extra
1 teaspoon salt
1/4 teaspoon paprika
pinch of chilli powder
1 cup (250 g/8 oz) plain yoghurt
red food colouring
lime wedges, to serve

1 Trim any excess fat from the chicken. Place in a large shallow dish. Brush with lemon juice, cover, and refrigerate for 30 minutes.
2 Process the coriander, cumin, onion, garlic, ginger, extra lemon juice and salt in a food processor to a smooth paste. Mix in the paprika, chilli, yoghurt and a few drops of food colouring until smooth and pink.
3 Coat the chicken with the tandoori mixture. Cover and refrigerate for at least 4 hours.
4 Preheat the oven to moderate 180°C (350°F/Gas 4). Place the chicken on a wire rack over a large baking dish. Bake for 45 minutes, without turning, until the chicken is cooked through.

NUTRITION PER SERVE (6)
Protein 20 g; Fat 6 g; Carbohydrate 3 g; Dietary Fibre 0 g; Cholesterol 70 mg; 645 kJ (155 cal)

COOK'S FILE

You can add extra food colouring to the yoghurt mixture if you prefer the traditional deep red tandoori colour.

VEAL WITH COCONUT SAUCE

Preparation time: 30 minutes + overnight marinating
Total cooking time: 1 hour 45 minutes
Serves 6

2 kg (4 lb) veal shanks, cut into short pieces (ask your butcher to do this)
4 cm (1½ inches) piece fresh ginger, grated
5 cloves garlic, crushed
3 tablespoons peanut oil
3 onions, chopped
1 tablespoon ground cumin
1 teaspoon ground turmeric
1 tablespoon poppy seeds
1½ teaspoons finely chopped red chilli
2½ cups (225 g/7¼ oz) desiccated coconut
5 cardamom pods, bruised
2 teaspoons ground cinnamon
2 tablespoons ground almonds
3 cups (750 ml/24 fl oz) water
500 g (1 lb) sweet potato, chopped

1 Combine the veal with the ginger and garlic in a bowl; cover and refrigerate overnight.
2 Heat half of the oil in a large pan, add the onion and cook over medium heat for about 10 minutes, until soft and golden. Remove from the pan. Brown the veal in batches over high heat in the remaining oil and set aside.
3 Add the cumin, turmeric, poppy seeds and chilli to the pan. Cook, stirring, for 2 minutes. Add the coconut, cardamom, cinnamon, almonds, veal and onion. Cook for 2 minutes, turning the veal regularly, until the mixture is soft and golden.
4 Add the water and bring to the boil, then simmer, covered, for 1 hour, stirring occasionally. Add the sweet potato and cook for 15 minutes, then remove the lid and cook for a further 15 minutes, until the meat is very tender and the sauce has reduced and thickened slightly. Season with salt and freshly ground black pepper.

NUTRITION PER SERVE
Protein 80 g; Fat 40 g; Carbohydrate 20 g; Dietary Fibre 10 g; Cholesterol 275 mg; 3120 kJ (740 cal)

Combine the veal with the ginger and garlic in a bowl.

Cook the onions over medium heat until soft and golden.

Cook the mixture for 2 minutes, turning the veal regularly.

Add the sweet potato to the pan and cook for a further 15 minutes.

CURRIED BEEF AND VEGETABLE PIES

Preparation time: 30 minutes
Total cooking time: 1 hour 30 minutes
Serves 6

3 tablespoons oil
2 tablespoons Thai red curry paste
1 kg (2 lb) rump steak, thinly sliced
2 tablespoons fish sauce
1½ cups (375 ml/12 fl oz) coconut milk
500 g (1 lb) pumpkin
300 g (9⅔ oz) slender eggplant
3 small red chillies, sliced
2 sheets frozen puff pastry, thawed
1 cup (30 g/1 oz) basil leaves, shredded
1 egg, beaten

1 Heat the oil in a large pan. Add the curry paste and cook, stirring, for 2 minutes. Add the beef, toss to coat in the curry paste, and stir-fry until browned. Stir in the fish sauce and coconut milk. Bring to the boil, and simmer, covered, for 30 minutes.

2 Preheat the oven to moderately hot 200°C (400°F/Gas 6). Cut the pumpkin into small cubes and cut the eggplant into thin slices. Add to the pan with the chilli and cook for a further 15 minutes.

3 Cut rounds from the pastry large enough to cover the tops of six 1-cup capacity ovenproof ramekins. Stir the basil into the beef mixture and spoon into the ramekins. Place the pastry rounds on top, and press around the edges. Brush with beaten egg and bake for 20–25 minutes, until puffed and golden brown.

NUTRITION PER SERVE
Protein 50 g; Fat 45 g; Carbohydrate 30 g; Dietary Fibre 3 g; Cholesterol 155 mg; 2940 kJ (700 cal)

Coat the beef with the curry paste and stir-fry until browned.

Thickly slice the pumpkin and cut into small cubes.

Cut rounds from the pastry large enough to cover the tops of the ramekins.

FRAGRANT FISH CURRY

Preparation time: 35 minutes
Total cooking time: 20 minutes
Serves 4–6

1 tablespoon vegetable oil
2 tablespoons Thai green curry paste
2 kaffir lime leaves
¼ cup (60 ml/2 fl oz) lime juice
1 tablespoon grated palm sugar
1½ cups (375 ml/12 fl oz) coconut milk
2 teaspoons fish sauce
500 g (1 lb/16 oz) firm white fish fillets cut into bite-sized pieces
200 g (6½ oz) calamari rings
150 g (4¾ oz) large raw prawns, peeled and deveined, tails intact
¼ cup (15 g/½ oz) chopped fresh coriander
2 tablespoons chopped fresh basil
150 g (4¾ oz) bamboo shoots

1 Heat the oil in a large pan, add the curry paste and cook over medium heat for 2–3 minutes. Add the kaffir lime leaves, juice, palm sugar and coconut milk. Bring to the boil, reduce the heat and simmer for 2–3 minutes. Season with the fish sauce.
2 Add the fish fillets and cook for 3 minutes. Add the calamari and the prawns and cook for a further 3–4 minutes, or until tender.
3 Add the coriander, basil and bamboo shoots. Stir well to combine and serve immediately with rice or on a bed of noodles.

NUTRITION PER SERVE (6)
Protein 30 g; Fat 20 g; Carbohydrate 8 g; Dietary Fibre 0 g; Cholesterol 160 mg; 1450 kJ (345 cal)

Add the lime leaves and juice, palm sugar and coconut milk.

Add the calamari rings and prawns to the pan.

Add the chopped coriander, basil and bamboo shoots just before serving.

CURRIED SWEET POTATO AND CARROT SOUP

Preparation time: 20 minutes
Total cooking time: 40 minutes
Serves 6–8

2 tablespoons vegetable oil
1 large onion, chopped
2 tablespoons curry powder
1 teaspoon cumin powder
1 kg (2¼ lb) sweet potato, peeled and diced
155 g (5 oz) carrots, diced
5 cups (1¼ litres) vegetable stock

1 Heat the oil in a large pan and add the onion, curry powder and cumin. Cook over medium heat for 5 minutes until the onion begins to soften but not brown. Add the sweet potato and carrot and cook for a further 5 minutes, stirring constantly.
2 Add the stock and bring to the boil. Reduce the heat and simmer for 30 minutes, or until the vegetables are tender. Remove from the heat and allow to cool. Place a little at a time in a food processor and blend until smooth. (If the mixture is too thick, add more stock or water.)
3 Return the soup to the pan and season to taste. Gently reheat and serve with sour cream and a sprinkling of cumin and a sprig of basil, if preferred.

NUTRITION PER SERVE (8)
Protein 4 g; Fat 5 g; Carbohydrate 20 g; Dietary Fibre 4 g; Cholesterol 0 mg; 630 kJ (150 cal)

Add the sweet potato and carrot to the onion mixture in the pan.

Process a little of the mixture at a time in a food processor until smooth.

Return the soup to the pan and season to taste with salt and pepper.

Fragrant Fish Curry (top) with Curried Sweet Potato and Carrot Soup

CURRIED LEMON LAMB

Preparation time: 15 minutes
+ 2 hours marinating
Total cooking time: 20 minutes
Serves 4

Marinade
1/4 cup (60 ml/2 fl oz) olive oil
1/2 teaspoon garam masala
1/4 teaspoon ground cinnamon
2 teaspoons ground coriander
2 teaspoons ground cumin
1 teaspoon ground turmeric
2 cloves garlic, crushed
1 tablespoon grated lemon rind
1/2 cup (125 ml/4 fl oz) lemon juice

500 g (1 lb) lamb fillets
2 tablespoons oil
3/4 cup (185 ml/6 fl oz) boiling water
1 cup (185 g/6 oz) couscous
30 g (1 oz) butter

1 To make Marinade: Mix all the ingredients in a bowl. Coat the lamb with the Marinade in a shallow dish. Cover; refrigerate for at least 2 hours.
2 Preheat the oven to moderate 180°C (350°F/Gas 4). Remove the lamb from the dish, reserving the marinade. Heat the oil in a pan and brown the lamb. Transfer to a baking dish, cover with the marinade and cook in the oven for 15 minutes, or until the lamb is tender.
3 Add the water to the couscous in a heatproof bowl. Cover tightly; set aside for 3–5 minutes, until all the liquid has been absorbed. Add the butter. Thinly slice the lamb. Serve on the couscous, with the marinade juices spooned over.

NUTRITION PER SERVE
Protein 30 g; Fat 35 g; Carbohydrate 25 g; Dietary Fibre 1 g; Cholesterol 100 mg; 2235 kJ (530 cal)

Turn the lamb fillets in the marinade to coat them thoroughly.

Brown the lamb on all sides by turning the meat as it cooks.

Add butter to the couscous and fluff up the grains with a fork.

Chop 1 tablespoon of fresh galangal with a sharp knife.

Heat the oil in a pan and stir-fry the Curry Paste for 2 minutes.

Add the zucchini, eggplant, pumpkin and green beans to the pan.

Add the noodles to a large pan of boiling water and cook until tender.

HOT VEGETABLE CURRY WITH SPICED NOODLES

Preparation time: 40 minutes
Total cooking time: 35 minutes
Serves 4–6

Curry Paste
5 red chillies, seeded and chopped
1 stem lemon grass, sliced
1 tablespoon chopped galangal
2 garlic cloves, crushed
1 small onion, chopped
1 tablespoon chopped fresh coriander
10 black peppercorns
2 tablespoons lime juice
1/2 teaspoon shrimp paste
2 teaspoons oil

2 tablespoons oil
1 1/2 cups (375 ml/12 fl oz) coconut milk
200 g (6 1/2 oz) green beans, cut into short lengths
2 small zucchini, thickly sliced
1 eggplant, cubed
200 g (6 1/2 oz) pumpkin, cubed
2 teaspoons fish sauce
5 kaffir lime leaves
2 tablespoons lime juice
1/4 cup (15 g/1/2 oz) chopped fresh coriander
1/2 cup (30 g/1 oz) chopped fresh basil

Spiced Noodles
2 tablespoons oil
1 small brown onion, chopped
1 clove garlic, crushed
1/2–1 teaspoon dried chilli flakes
1/2 teaspoon garam masala
200 g (6 1/2 oz) thin egg noodles

1 To make Curry Paste: Blend all the ingredients in a food processor to a smooth paste.

2 Heat the oil in a pan and stir-fry the Curry Paste for 2 minutes. Add the coconut milk and 1/2 cup (125 ml/4 fl oz) water; bring to the boil. Reduce the heat and add the vegetables, fish sauce, kaffir lime leaves and juice. Cook, covered, until tender. Stir through the coriander and basil.

3 To make Spiced Noodles: Heat the oil in a pan. Cook the onion and garlic over medium–low heat for 5 minutes. Add the chilli flakes and garam masala; cook for 2 minutes. Meanwhile, cook the noodles in boiling water until tender and drain. Add to the onion mixture and toss to combine.

NUTRITION PER SERVE (6)
Protein 5 g; Fat 25 g; Carbohydrate 15 g; Dietary Fibre 5 g; Cholesterol 0 mg; 1415 kJ (335 cal)

CURRY PUFFS WITH YOGHURT AND MINT SAUCE

Preparation time: 40 minutes
Total cooking time: 40 minutes
Makes 16

2 tablespoons vegetable oil
1 tablespoon curry powder
250 g (8 oz) pork mince
1 cup (165 g/5½ oz) finely chopped potato
1 cup (155 g/5 oz) finely chopped pumpkin
1 cup (155 g/5 oz) finely chopped carrot
2 tablespoons chopped spring onions
1 large brown onion, chopped
4 sheets frozen puff pastry

Yoghurt and Mint Sauce
1½ cups (375 g/12 oz) plain yoghurt
¼ cup (15 g/½ oz) chopped mint
2 garlic cloves, crushed

1 Preheat the oven to hot 220°C (425°F/Gas 7). Brush two oven trays with melted butter or oil. Heat the oil in a frying pan and cook the curry powder, stirring, for 1 minute. Add the mince and cook over high heat for 5 minutes, until browned. Break up any lumps with a fork as it cooks.
2 Add the vegetables; cook, stirring, for 2 minutes. Add ½ cup (125 ml/4 fl oz) water, reduce the heat to medium, and cook, covered, until the vegetables are tender. Remove the lid and cook until any liquid has evaporated. Season well and set aside to cool.
3 Cut 4 triangles out of each pastry sheet. Divide the mixture between the triangles. Fold over and press the edges together, pinching in a fluted pattern to seal. Place the Puffs onto the trays and bake for 20 minutes, until puffed and golden brown.
4 To make Yoghurt and Mint Sauce: Place all the ingredients in a bowl and whisk together. Season with salt and freshly ground black pepper.

NUTRITION PER SERVE
Protein 10 g; Fat 15 g; Carbohydrate 20 g; Dietary Fibre 2 g; Cholesterol 20 mg; 955 kJ (225 cal)

Cook the mince until browned, breaking up any lumps with a fork.

Season the mixture to taste before setting aside to cool.

Fold the pastry over to enclose the filling, then press the edges together to seal.

Whisk together the yoghurt, mint and garlic in a bowl.

MADRAS CURRY

Preparation time: 20 minutes
Total cooking time: 1 hour 10 minutes
Serves 4

3 tablespoons ground coriander
1½ tablespoons ground cumin
1 teaspoon brown mustard seeds
½ teaspoon cracked black peppercorns
1 teaspoon chilli powder
1 teaspoon ground turmeric
1 teaspoon salt
2 teaspoons crushed garlic
2 teaspoons grated fresh ginger
3–4 tablespoons white vinegar
1 tablespoon oil or ghee
1 onion, chopped
1 kg (2 lb) skirt or chuck steak, cubed
¼ cup (60 g/2 oz) tomato paste
1 cup (250 ml/8 fl oz) beef stock

1 Combine the coriander, cumin, mustard seeds, peppercorns, chilli powder, turmeric, salt, garlic and ginger in a small bowl. Add the vinegar and mix to form a paste.

2 Heat the oil or ghee in a large pan. Cook the onion until golden, then add the curry paste and cook, stirring, for 1 minute further. Add the steak and cook, stirring, until well coated with the onion mixture.

3 Add the tomato paste and stock. Bring just to the boil, reduce the heat and simmer, covered, for 1 hour, or until the meat is tender. Garnish with extra mustard seeds.

NUTRITION PER SERVE
Protein 55 g; Fat 15 g; Carbohydrate 4 g; Dietary Fibre 1 g; Cholesterol 180 mg; 1440 kJ (340 cal)

Add the vinegar to the spice mixture and mix to a smooth paste.

When the onion is golden, add the curry paste and cook for 1 minute further.

Add the tomato paste and stock to the pan before bringing to the boil.

INDIAN PRAWN CURRY

Preparation time: 25 minutes
Total cooking time: 20 minutes
Serves 4

25 g (3/4 oz) ghee or butter
1 onion, finely chopped
3 cloves garlic, crushed
1 teaspoon grated fresh ginger
1/2 teaspoon cayenne pepper
2 teaspoons ground cumin
1 teaspoon garam masala
1/2 teaspoon ground turmeric
1 kg (2 lb) raw prawns, peeled and deveined, tails left intact
425 g (13 1/2 oz) can chopped tomatoes, undrained
1/3 cup (80 ml/2 3/4 fl oz) coconut cream
2 teaspoons finely chopped green chilli
2 tablespoons chopped fresh coriander

1 Heat the ghee or butter in a large, deep frying pan. Add the onion and gently cook over medium heat until soft and golden. Add the garlic and ginger and cook for 1 minute. Add the cayenne pepper, cumin, garam masala and turmeric and cook for 1 minute further, or until fragrant.

2 Add the prawns and tomatoes to the pan and simmer for 10–15 minutes, or until the prawns are cooked and the liquid has reduced.

3 Stir in the coconut cream. Add the chilli a little at a time until the mixture is as hot as you like. Season to taste with salt, and serve scattered with the coriander.

NUTRITION PER SERVE
Protein 25 g; Fat 10 g; Carbohydrate 5 g; Dietary Fibre 3 g; Cholesterol 255 mg; 925 kJ (220 cal)

COOK'S FILE

Note: You can substitute white fish fillets for half or all the prawns.

Wear rubber gloves when chopping chillies to protect against burning.

Cook the chopped onion over medium heat until soft and golden.

Add the spices to the pan and cook for 1 minute, or until fragrant.

Bring the water, milk, onion and spice mixture to the boil and stir in the rice.

Cut the seafood into bite-size pieces with a sharp knife.

Cook the onion and spices over medium heat until the onion is soft.

Add the coconut milk and curry leaves to the pan and bring to the boil.

SQUID AND OCTOPUS CURRY WITH AROMATIC RICE

Preparation time: 30 minutes
Total cooking time: 45 minutes
Serves 6

Aromatic Rice

3/4 cup (185 ml/6 fl oz) coconut milk
1/4 teaspoon ground turmeric
1/2 teaspoon ground cumin
1/2 teaspoon cinnamon
2 teaspoons chopped fresh ginger
2 cloves garlic, chopped
1 small onion, finely chopped
1 cup (200 g/6 1/2 oz) basmati rice

300 g (9 2/3 oz) cleaned squid
300 g (9 2/3 oz) cleaned octopus
2 tablespoons oil
1 large onion, chopped
3 cloves garlic, finely chopped
1 teaspoon grated fresh ginger
1 teaspoon sambal oelek
2 teaspoons ground cumin
2 teaspoons ground turmeric
2 teaspoons grated lemon rind
2 cups (500 ml/16 fl oz) coconut milk
5 curry leaves
1 tablespoon dark brown sugar
1/4 cup lemon juice
lemon wedges, to serve

1 **To make Aromatic Rice:** Place all the ingredients except the rice in a large pan with 1 cup (250 ml/4 fl oz) water. Bring to the boil. Stir in the rice, reduce the heat and simmer, covered, for 20 minutes.
2 Cut the seafood into bite-size pieces.
3 Heat the oil; cook the onion, garlic, ginger, sambal oelek, cumin, turmeric and lemon rind for 5 minutes over medium heat, or until the onion is soft.
4 Add the coconut milk and curry leaves. Bring to the boil then reduce the heat and simmer for 15 minutes. Add the seafood, sugar and lemon juice. Simmer for 2 minutes or until the seafood is just tender. Serve over the Aromatic Rice.

NUTRITION PER SERVE
Protein 20 g; Fat 30 g; Carbohydrate 35 g; Dietary Fibre 2 g; Cholesterol 100 mg; 2070 kJ (490 cal)

BOMBAY CURRY

Preparation time: 20 minutes
Total cooking time: 1 hour 30 minutes
Serves 4–6

1 kg (2 lb) chuck steak
1 tablespoon ghee or oil
2 onions, chopped
2 cloves garlic, crushed
2 green chillies, chopped
1 tablespoon grated fresh ginger
1½ teaspoons ground turmeric
1 teaspoon ground cumin
1 tablespoon ground coriander
½–1 teaspoon chilli powder
1 teaspoon salt
400 g (12⅔ oz) can tomatoes
1 cup (250 ml/8 fl oz) coconut milk

1 Cut the beef into cubes. Heat the ghee or oil in a large pan and cook the onion until just soft.

2 Add the garlic, chilli, ginger, turmeric, cumin, coriander and chilli powder. Stir until heated; add the beef and cook, stirring, over high heat until well coated with the spice mixture.

3 Add the salt and tomatoes. Simmer, covered, for 1–1½ hours, or until the beef is tender. Stir in the coconut milk and simmer, uncovered, for a further 5–10 minutes, or until slightly thickened. Garnish with fresh ginger.

NUTRITION PER SERVE (6)
Protein 35 g; Fat 15 g; Carbohydrate 5 g; Dietary Fibre 2 g; Cholesterol 120 mg; 1325 kJ (315 cal)

COOK'S FILE

Note: Bombay Curry is best made 1–2 days in advance. Store, covered, in the refrigerator.

Cut the beef into cubes, trimming any excess fat from the meat.

Add the garlic, chilli, ginger, turmeric, cumin, coriander and chilli powder.

Stir in the salt and tomatoes, then simmer, covered, until the meat is tender.

CHICKPEA CURRY

Preparation time: 10 minutes
Total Cooking time: 40 minutes
Serves 4

1 tablespoon ghee or oil
2 onions, sliced
4 cloves garlic, crushed
1 teaspoon chilli powder
1 teaspoon salt
1 teaspoon ground turmeric
1 teaspoon paprika
1 tablespoon ground cumin
1 tablespoon ground coriander
880 g (1 lb 12²/3 oz) can chickpeas, rinsed and drained
440 g (14 oz) can chopped tomatoes
1 teaspoon garam masala

1 Heat the ghee or oil in a pan. Add the onion and garlic; cook, stirring, until the onion is soft. Add the chilli powder, salt, turmeric, paprika, cumin and coriander. Cook, stirring, for 2–3 minutes.

2 Stir in the chickpeas and tomato. Simmer, covered, over low heat for 20 minutes, stirring occasionally.

3 Stir in the garam masala. Simmer, covered, for a further 10 minutes. Serve as part of an Indian meal with paratha.

NUTRITION PER SERVE
Protein 45 g; Fat 20 g; Carbohydrate 120 g; Dietary Fibre 35 g; Cholesterol 15 mg; 3315 kJ (790 cal)

Add the chilli powder, salt, turmeric, paprika, cumin and coriander to the pan.

Add the rinsed and drained chickpeas, and chopped tomatoes.

Stir in 1 teaspoon of garam masala and then simmer, covered, for 10 minutes.

BEEF RENDANG

Preparation time: 25 minutes
Total cooking time: 1 hour 30 minutes
Serves 4–6

2 onions, chopped
4 cloves garlic, crushed
3 red chillies, seeded and chopped
2 green chillies, chopped
1 tablespoon grated fresh ginger
2 cups (500 ml/16 fl oz) coconut milk
1 tablespoon oil
1 tablespoon ground coriander
1 tablespoon ground cumin
1 teaspoon ground cinnamon
1 teaspoon ground turmeric
1/4 teaspoon ground cloves
1/4 teaspoon chilli powder
1 large strip of lemon rind
1 kg (2 lb) chuck or skirt steak, cubed
1 tablespoon lemon juice
1 tablespoon brown sugar
1 teaspoon tamarind concentrate

1 Process half the onion, the garlic, chilli, ginger and 2 tablespoons of coconut milk in a food processor until the mixture forms a paste.
2 Heat the oil in a pan; add the paste, remaining onion, coriander, cumin, cinnamon, turmeric, cloves, chilli powder, rind, steak and remaining coconut milk. Mix well to coat the meat. Bring to the boil; reduce the heat and simmer, stirring occasionally, for 1 1/2 hours or until the meat is tender and the mixture is almost dry.
3 When the oil starts to separate from the gravy, add the lemon juice, sugar and tamarind and stir until heated through. Serve with rice and sprinkle with chilli flakes, if preferred.

NUTRITION PER SERVE (6)
Protein 35 g; Fat 25 g; Carbohydrate 8 g; Dietary Fibre 1 g; Cholesterol 110 mg; 1670 kJ (395 cal)

Process the onion, garlic, chilli, ginger and coconut milk into a paste.

Make sure the meat is well coated with the sauce, then bring to the boil.

Add the lemon juice, tamarind and sugar, and stir until heated through.

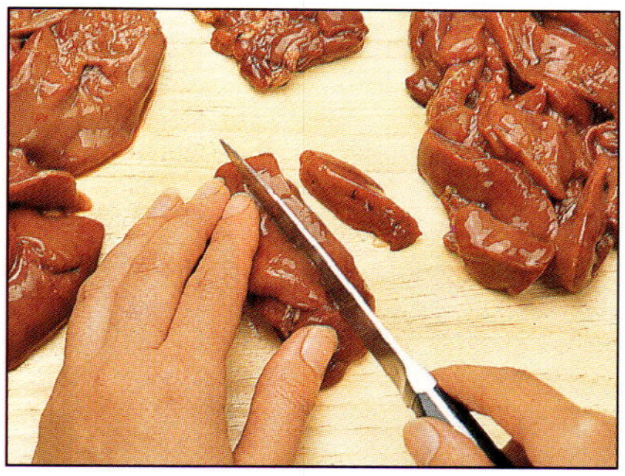

Trim and slice the chicken livers, making sure to remove any membrane.

Mix together the marinade ingredients and then pour over the livers to coat.

Sprinkle the coriander and cumin over the liver and season well.

Add the chicken stock and snow peas, then simmer gently for 2–3 minutes.

SPICED LIVER CURRY

Preparation time: 25 minutes
+ 2 hours marinating
Total cooking time: 18 minutes
Serves 4

3 tablespoons dark soy sauce
3 cloves garlic, crushed
1 tablespoon sesame seeds, toasted
1 teaspoon sesame oil
500 g (1 lb) chicken livers, trimmed and sliced
2 tablespoons olive oil
1 onion, sliced
1 red capsicum, sliced
1 teaspoon ground coriander
1 teaspoon ground cumin
2 tablespoons peanut oil
1/2 cup (125 ml/4 fl oz) chicken stock
100 g (3 1/3 oz) snow peas, trimmed

1 Combine the soy sauce, garlic, sesame seeds and sesame oil with 2 tablespoons water. Place the livers in a dish and pour over the marinade. Cover and refrigerate for 2 hours.
2 Heat half the olive oil in a large, heavy-based pan and cook the onion and capsicum over medium-low heat for 5–10 minutes, or until softened. Remove from the pan and set aside.
3 Sprinkle the liver with coriander and cumin and season well with freshly ground black pepper. Remove from the dish, reserving the marinade.
4 Heat the remaining olive oil and the peanut oil in a pan and add the liver. Cook over high heat, turning often, for about 3–5 minutes, until firm but still slightly pink inside. Return the onion, capsicum and reserved marinade to the pan. Add the stock and snow peas; simmer gently for 2–3 minutes. Serve immediately, with rice if desired. Garnish with toasted sesame seeds.

NUTRITION PER SERVE
Protein 35 g; Fat 35 g; Carbohydrate 5 g; Dietary Fibre 2 g; Cholesterol 705 mg; 2042 kJ (485 cal)

LAMB KOFTA

Preparation time: 30 minutes
Total cooking time: 50 minutes
Serves 4–6

1 kg (2 lb) lamb mince
1 onion, finely chopped
2 green chillies, chopped
3 teaspoons grated fresh ginger
3 cloves garlic, crushed
1 teaspoon ground cardamom
1 egg
1/3 cup (25 g/3/4 oz) fresh breadcrumbs
2 tablespoons ghee or oil

Sauce
1 tablespoon ghee or oil
1 onion, sliced
1 green chilli, chopped
3 teaspoons grated fresh ginger
2 cloves garlic, crushed
1 teaspoon ground turmeric
3 teaspoons ground coriander
2 teaspoons ground cumin
1 teaspoon chilli powder
2 tablespoons white vinegar
1 1/3 cups (350 ml/11 fl oz) water
3/4 cup (185 g/6 oz) plain yoghurt
1 1/4 cups (315 ml/10 fl oz) coconut milk

1 Line an oven tray with baking paper. Mix together the mince, onion, chilli, ginger, garlic, cardamom, egg and breadcrumbs. Season with salt and pepper and mix well. Roll level tablespoons of the mixture into balls and place on the tray.

2 Heat the ghee or oil in a pan. Cook the meatballs in two batches until browned all over. Set aside.

3 To make Sauce: Heat the ghee or oil in a pan. Add the onion, chilli, ginger, garlic and turmeric. Cook, stirring, over low heat until the onion is soft. Add the coriander, cumin, chilli powder, vinegar, water and meatballs and stir gently to combine. Cover and simmer for 30 minutes.

4 Combine the yoghurt and coconut milk and stir into the sauce. Simmer for a further 10 minutes, with the pan partially covered.

NUTRITION PER SERVE (6)
Protein 40 g; Fat 30 g; Carbohydrate 8 g; Dietary Fibre 2 g; Cholesterol 165 mg; 1895 kJ (450 cal)

Roll level tablespoons of the mixture into balls and place on the prepared tray.

Brown the meatballs in two batches, to prevent stewing.

Add the meatballs, spices, vinegar and water to the pan.

Add the combined yoghurt and coconut milk and stir until thoroughly combined.

MULLIGATAWNY

Preparation time: 30 minutes
Total cooking time: 1 hour 20 minutes
Serves 6

1 kg (2 lb) chicken pieces
2 tablespoons plain flour
2 teaspoons curry powder
1 teaspoon ground turmeric
1/2 teaspoon ground ginger
60 g (2 oz) butter
12 black peppercorns
6 whole cloves
6 cups (1.5 litres) chicken stock
1 large apple, peeled, cored and chopped
2 tablespoons lemon juice
1/2 cup (125 ml/4 fl oz) cream
steamed rice, to serve

1 Trim the chicken of excess fat and sinew. Combine the flour, curry powder, turmeric and ginger, and rub into the chicken.

2 Heat the butter in a large pan and cook the chicken until lightly browned on all sides. Tie the peppercorns and cloves in a small piece of muslin and add to the pan with the stock. Bring to the boil, reduce the heat slightly and simmer, covered, for 1 hour. Add the apple and cook for 15 minutes further.

3 Remove the chicken from the pan and discard the muslin bag. When cool enough, remove the skin from the chicken; finely shred the flesh. Skim any fat from the surface of the soup.

4 Return the chicken to the pan. Stir in the lemon juice and cream, and heat through gently. Garnish with thinly sliced ginger.

Combine the flour, curry powder, ginger and turmeric in a bowl.

Tie the cloves and peppercorns in a piece of muslin.

Finely shred the chicken flesh and discard the bones.

Stir in the lemon juice and cream and gently heat through.

NUTRITION PER SERVE
Protein 25 g; Fat 25 g; Carbohydrate 10 g; Dietary Fibre 1 g; Cholesterol 130 mg; 1405 kJ (440 cal)

CURRIED SUMMER FRUITS

Preparation time: 25 minutes
Total cooking time: 15 minutes
Serves 4

2 Granny Smith apples
1 small rockmelon
1/2 large pineapple
1/2 pawpaw
1 mango
2 large bananas
70 g (2 1/3 oz) dried dates, pitted
50 g (1 2/3 oz) ghee
3 cm (1 1/4 inches) fresh ginger, finely grated
1 1/2 tablespoons curry powder
4 spring onions, chopped
2 tablespoons lemon juice
50 g (1 2/3 oz) cashews, toasted
plain yoghurt, to serve

1 Peel all the fruits and cut into bite-size pieces. Roughly chop the dates.

2 Melt the ghee over low heat in a heavy-based pan. Gently cook the ginger, curry powder and spring onion for 3 minutes. Add the fruit and gently toss to coat in the mixture.

3 Cook gently for 7 minutes, or until the fruit just starts to soften. Add the lemon juice and stir gently. Serve with steamed rice, garnished with the cashews and yoghurt.

NUTRITION PER SERVE
Protein 10 g; Fat 20 g; Carbohydrate 80 g; Dietary Fibre 15 g; Cholesterol 35 mg; 2185 kJ (520 cal)

COOK'S FILE

Note: This dish is delicious served as a main meal or with a meat curry, grilled pork or chicken.

Cut the pawpaw, rockmelon, pineapple and mango into bite-size chunks.

Cook the ginger, curry powder and spring onion over low heat for 3 minutes.

Add the lemon juice to the pan and gently stir through.

Fry the saffron threads in a dry pan over low heat for 1–2 minutes.

Add the onion, garlic, ginger and chilli and stir to combine.

Add the saffron with its liquid, and the stock to the pan.

Reduce the stock over high heat until about 1 1/2 cups remain.

SAFFRON CHICKEN

Preparation time: 25 minutes
Total cooking time: 1 hour 20 minutes
Serves 6

1 teaspoon saffron threads
2 tablespoons hot water
2 tablespoons oil
2 onions, chopped
3 cloves garlic, crushed
3 cm (1 1/4 inch) piece fresh ginger, chopped
2 red chillies, seeded and sliced
1 teaspoon ground cardamom
1 teaspoon ground cumin
1/2 teaspoon ground turmeric
2 kg (4 lb) chicken pieces
2 cups (500 ml/16 fl oz) chicken stock

1 Fry the saffron threads in a dry frying pan over low heat for 1–2 minutes. Transfer to a small bowl, add the hot water and set aside.
2 Heat the oil in a pan over medium heat; add the onion, garlic, ginger and chilli. Cover and cook for 10 minutes, or until very soft.
3 Add the spices, and cook over medium heat for 2 minutes. Add the chicken and cook over high heat for 3 minutes, or until the meat is well coated. Add the saffron liquid and the stock. Bring to the boil, then reduce the heat, and cook, covered, stirring occasionally, for 30 minutes.
4 Uncover, and cook for a further 20 minutes. Remove the chicken and keep warm. Reduce the stock to about 1 1/2 cups (375 ml/12 fl oz) over very high heat. Pour over the chicken. Season with salt and pepper, to taste.

NUTRITION PER SERVE
Protein 45 g; Fat 15 g; Carbohydrate 3 g; Dietary Fibre 1 g; Cholesterol 155 mg; 1445 kJ (345 cal)

AROMATIC LAMB CURRY

Preparation time: 30 minutes
+ 1 hour marinating
Total cooking time: 1 hour
Serves 4–6

2 kg (4 lb) leg of lamb, boned
1 onion, chopped
2 teaspoons grated fresh ginger
3 cloves garlic
1 tablespoon coriander seeds
2 teaspoons ground cumin
1 teaspoon cardamom pods
1/2 teaspoon salt
good pinch of cayenne pepper
2 tablespoons ghee or oil
1 onion, extra, sliced
2 tablespoons tomato paste
1/2 cup (125 g/4 oz) thick, plain yoghurt

1 Remove all the excess fat, skin and sinew from the lamb. Cut the meat into cubes and place in a large bowl. Process the onion, ginger, garlic, coriander seeds, cumin, cardamom pods, salt and pepper in a food processor bowl until the mixture becomes a smooth paste.
2 Add the spice mixture to the lamb and mix well to coat. Cover and refrigerate for 1 hour.
3 Heat the ghee or oil in a large pan; add the extra onion and cook, stirring, until soft. Add the lamb mixture and stir over high heat for 8–10 minutes, or until the lamb is browned and the liquid has evaporated. Reduce the heat; add the tomato paste and 2 tablespoons of yoghurt and stir until combined. Simmer until almost dry.
4 Stir in the remaining yoghurt, 2 tablespoons at a time, until the mixture is nearly dry between each addition. Cover the pan and simmer over low heat for 30 minutes, or until the meat is tender, stirring occasionally. Add a little water if the mixture is too dry.

NUTRITION PER SERVE (6)
Protein 50 g; Fat 15 g; Carbohydrate 4 g; Dietary Fibre 1 g; Cholesterol 170 mg; 1510 kJ (360 cal)

COOK'S FILE

Note: Try to choose a brand of yoghurt that is thick and creamy, as a thinner yoghurt may curdle.

Trim the skin, sinew and excess fat from the lamb and cut into cubes.

Add the spice mixture to the lamb and mix well to coat.

Add the tomato paste and 2 tablespoons of the yoghurt to the pan.

Cook until the meat is tender and the curry is dry.

THAI GREEN CHICKEN CURRY

Preparation time: 20 minutes
Total cooking time: 25 minutes
Serves 4

1 tablespoon oil
1 onion, chopped
1–2 tablespoons Thai green curry paste
1 1/2 cups (375 ml/12 fl oz) coconut milk
1/2 cup (125 ml/4 fl oz) water
500 g (1 lb) chicken thigh fillets, cut into bite-size pieces
100 g (3 1/3 oz) green beans, cut in half
6 kaffir lime leaves, shredded
1 tablespoon fish sauce
1 tablespoon lime juice
1 teaspoon finely grated lime rind
2 teaspoons soft brown sugar
1/4 cup (7 g/1/4 oz) fresh coriander leaves

1 Heat the oil in a wok or heavy-based pan. Add the onion and curry paste, and cook for about 1 minute, stirring constantly. Add the combined coconut milk and water and bring to the boil.
2 Add the chicken, beans and kaffir lime leaves and stir to combine. Simmer for 15–20 minutes, or until the chicken is tender.
3 Stir in the fish sauce, lime juice, rind and brown sugar until well combined. Sprinkle with the coriander leaves and serve with steamed rice.

NUTRITION PER SERVE
Protein 30 g; Fat 35 g; Carbohydrate 10 g; Dietary Fibre 1 g; Cholesterol 85 mg; 1895 kJ (450 cal)

Add the combined coconut milk and water to the onion mixture.

Add the chicken pieces, beans and kaffir lime leaves; stir to combine.

Stir in the fish sauce, lime juice, rind and brown sugar until well combined.

CURRIED CHICKEN PIE

Preparation time: 40 minutes
Total cooking time: 1 hour
Serves 6

Pastry
2 cups (250 g/8 oz) plain flour
1 teaspoon ground turmeric
1 teaspoon ground cumin
125 g (4 oz) butter, cut into small cubes
1 egg, lightly beaten
2–3 tablespoons cold water

1 cooked chicken (barbecued or poached)
40 g (1 3/4 oz) butter, extra
1 onion, peeled and chopped
2 tablespoons curry powder
1 teaspoon cumin seeds
1 tablespoon flour
1 1/2 cups (375 ml/12 fl oz) chicken stock
1/2 cup (125 ml/4 fl oz) cream
1 tablespoon mango chutney
200 g (6 1/2 oz) sweet potato, cubed and cooked
milk, for glazing

1 To make Pastry: Place the flour, turmeric, cumin and butter in a food processor. Process the mixture for about 15 seconds until fine and crumbly. Add the egg and enough water to bring the mixture together. Turn out onto a lightly floured surface and press together until smooth. Cover with plastic wrap and refrigerate for 20 minutes while making the filling.

2 Remove the skin and bones from the chicken and chop the meat into bite-size pieces. Heat the butter in a large pan or deep frying pan and cook the onion until soft and transparent. Add the curry powder and cumin seeds and cook for about 1 minute longer.

3 Add the flour and cook for another 30 seconds. Remove from the heat and stir in the stock gradually, making sure the mixture is smooth between each addition. Return to the heat and cook, stirring, until the sauce bubbles and thickens. Add the cream, mango chutney, sweet potato and chicken meat. Simmer for 5 minutes, then season to taste with salt and black pepper. Remove from the heat and cool completely. Preheat the oven to moderately hot 190°C (375°F/Gas 5).

4 Divide the pastry into two portions. Roll out one half on a lightly floured surface until it is large enough to cover the base and sides of a 23 cm (9 inch) pie dish. Line the dish with the pastry and spoon the chicken mixture into the base.

5 Roll out the remaining pastry to cover the top of the pie. Brush the adjoining edges with water and press together. Trim the edges with a sharp knife. Roll out the trimmings and cut into decorative shapes. Brush the underneath of the shapes with milk and press gently on to the pie.

6 Brush the top of the pie with milk and bake for 40 minutes, until the top is golden brown. Serve hot or at room temperature.

NUTRITION PER SERVE
Protein 30 g; Fat 50 g; Carbohydrate 40 g; Dietary Fibre 5 g; Cholesterol 240 mg; 2795 kJ (710 cal)

COOK'S FILE

Note: It is very important that the filling is cold when added to the pastry, otherwise it will cause the pastry to become soggy.

Add the egg and enough water to bring the mixture together.

After removing the skin and bones, chop the chicken meat into bite-size pieces.

As you stir in the stock, make sure the mixture is smooth between each addition.

Spoon the chicken mixture into the base of the pie.

Seal the adjoining edges of the pie and trim with a sharp knife.

Brush the top of the pie with milk before placing in the oven.

CURRIED ZUCCHINI

Preparation time: 15 minutes
Total cooking time: 25 minutes
Serves 4

500 g (1 lb) zucchini
1 tablespoon oil
1 large onion, finely chopped
2 teaspoons ground cumin
1 teaspoon ground coriander
1 tablespoon garam masala
1/2 cup (125 ml/4 fl oz) vegetable stock or water
1 teaspoon grated lemon rind
2 ripe tomatoes, finely chopped

1 Halve the zucchini lengthways, and cut into large pieces.
2 Heat the oil in a deep heavy-based pan and cook the onion over low heat. Add the cumin, coriander and 3 teaspoons of garam masala. Cook, stirring, for 2 minutes.
3 Toss the zucchini through the spice paste. Add the vegetable stock or water and lemon rind and bring to the boil. Reduce the heat and simmer, covered, for 10 minutes. Add the tomato and remaining masala and stir through. Season with salt and pepper. Serve as a side dish with curries, rice, yoghurts and chutneys. For a variation, substitute trimmed okra for zucchini.

NUTRITION PER SERVE
Protein 3 g; Fat 5 g; Carbohydrate 5 g; Dietary Fibre 4 g; Cholesterol 0 mg; 345 kJ (80 cal)

Halve the zucchini lengthways and cut into pieces about 5 cm (2 inches) long.

Cook the onion and the spices until they are very aromatic.

Stir through the tomato until the mixture is well combined.

THAI DUCK CURRY

Preparation time: 40 minutes
Total cooking time: 1 hour 20 minutes
Serves 4

1 duck (about 1.5 kg/3 lb)
1 onion, finely chopped
2 tablespoons red curry paste
1 1/2 cups (375 ml/12 fl oz) thin coconut milk
4 kaffir lime leaves, shredded
1/2 cup (90 g/3 oz) canned sliced bamboo shoots
1 1/2 tablespoons fish sauce
2 teaspoons soft brown sugar

1 Preheat the oven to moderately hot 200°C (400°F/Gas 6). Cut the duck in half by cutting down either side of the backbone. Cut each half into 4 pieces. Discard the backbone and any large pieces of fat inside the carcass or attached to the back legs. Wash the duck and pat dry with paper towels. Pierce the skin a couple of times on each piece. Place the meat on a rack above a baking dish filled to a depth of about 2 cm (3/4 inch) with water. Cook in the oven for 45 minutes, or until the skin is golden and crisp.
2 Cook the onion, curry paste and coconut milk in a wok or heavy-based pan over medium heat for 8 minutes. Stir in 1 1/2 cups (375 ml/12 fl oz) water and add the duck pieces. Bring to the boil, turning the duck regularly in the sauce. Add the lime leaves, reduce the heat and simmer for about 30 minutes.
3 Add the bamboo shoots; season with the fish sauce and brown sugar. Serve with steamed rice and salad.

NUTRITION PER SERVE
Protein 25 g; Fat 80 g; Carbohydrate 10 g; Dietary Fibre 1 g; Cholesterol 140 mg; 3575 kJ (850 cal)

COOK'S FILE

Note: If you prefer, any oil that rises to the surface of the curry can be carefully lifted off with a spoon.

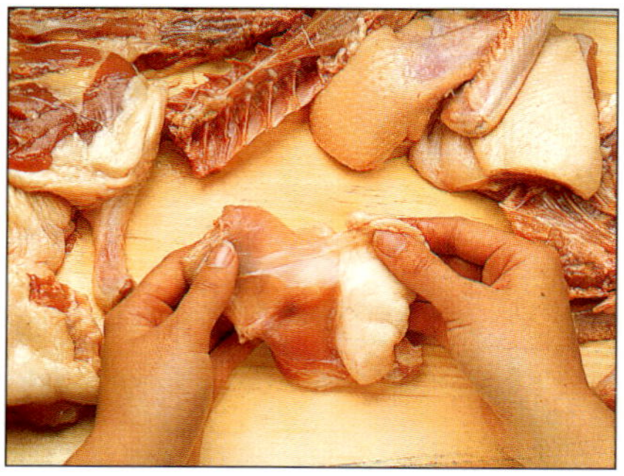
As you cut the duck, remove and discard any large pieces of fat.

Bring to the boil, turning the duck pieces regularly in the sauce.

Add the canned sliced bamboo shoots to the pan and season well.

Curried Zucchini (top) with Thai Duck Curry

ROGAN JOSH

Preparation time: 25 minutes
Total cooking time: 1 hour 30 minutes
Serves 4

1 tablespoon ghee
2 onions, chopped
1 teaspoon chilli powder
1 tablespoon ground coriander
2 teaspoons ground cumin
3 cloves garlic, crushed
1 tablespoon grated fresh ginger
1 teaspoon ground cardamom
½ teaspoon ground cloves
1 teaspoon ground turmeric
½ cup (125 g/4 oz) plain yoghurt
1 teaspoon salt
410 g (13 oz) can tomatoes
1 kg (2 lb) lamb, diced
3 teaspoons garam masala
¼ cup (30 g/1 oz) slivered almonds, toasted
fresh coriander leaves, to garnish

1 Heat the ghee in a large pan. Add the onion and cook, stirring, until soft and golden. Add the chilli powder, coriander, cumin, garlic, ginger, cardamom, cloves, turmeric and yoghurt. Stir until combined.

2 Add the salt and tomatoes and simmer for 5 minutes. Add the lamb and stir until coated. Cover and cook over low heat for 1–1½ hours, or until the lamb is tender.

3 Uncover and simmer until the liquid is almost all evaporated. Add the garam masala and stir until mixed through. Serve sprinkled with almonds and coriander.

NUTRITION PER SERVE
Protein 60 g; Fat 20 g; Carbohydrate 10 g; Dietary Fibre 3 g; Cholesterol 185 mg; 1905 kJ (455 cal)

Cook the onion in a large pan, stirring, until soft and golden.

Add the lamb to the sauce and stir until well coated.

Just before serving, add the garam masala and stir until mixed through.

Cook the masala paste over medium heat until the oil begins to separate.

Add the chilli powder, ginger and onion, and cook until the onion softens.

Stir in the tomato and stock, then bring the mixture to the boil.

Add the beans and cook for 10 minutes, or until all the vegetables are tender.

VEGETABLE CURRY

Preparation time: 25 minutes
Total cooking time: 50 minutes
Serves 4–6

2 tablespoons oil
2 tablespoons green masala paste
1 teaspoon chilli powder
1 tablespoon grated fresh ginger
1 onion, chopped
300 g (9 2/3 oz) cauliflower, cut into florets
300 g (9 2/3 oz) pumpkin, cubed
3 baby eggplants, cubed
2 carrots, cubed
3 tomatoes, peeled, seeded and chopped
1 1/2 cups (375 ml/12 fl oz) vegetable stock
125 g (4 oz) green beans, chopped

1 Heat the oil in a large heavy-based pan, and cook the masala paste over medium heat for 2 minutes, or until the oil starts to separate from the paste.
2 Add the chilli powder, ginger and onion and cook for 3 minutes.
3 Add the cauliflower, pumpkin, eggplant and carrot and stir to coat in the paste mixture. Stir in the tomato and stock. Bring to the boil, reduce the heat and simmer for 30 minutes
4 Add the beans and cook for 10 minutes, or until the vegetables are tender. Season well with salt and pepper, to taste. Serve with rice.

NUTRITION PER SERVE (6)
Protein 4 g; Fat 10 g; Carbohydrate 10 g; Dietary Fibre 5 g; Cholesterol 0 mg; 590 kJ (140 cal)

BEEF AND BABY SQUASH CURRY

Preparation time: 35 minutes
Total cooking time: 2 hours 25 minutes
Serves 4

800 g (1 lb 10 oz) gravy beef
200 g (6 1/2 oz) baby green squash
1 cup (155 g/5 oz) roughly chopped onion
4 cloves garlic, crushed
3 teaspoons finely chopped fresh ginger
1 teaspoon ground turmeric
1/2 teaspoon paprika
1/2 teaspoon chilli powder
4 tablespoons vegetable oil
2 tablespoons sesame oil
1 teaspoon ground cumin
1 1/2 cups (375 ml/12 fl oz) beef stock
2 tablespoons garlic chives, finely chopped
1 lemon, cut into wedges

1 Cut the beef into cubes. Trim the squash and cut in half vertically.
2 Place the onion, garlic, ginger, turmeric, paprika, chilli powder and 3 teaspoons of the vegetable oil in a food processor, and process until a thick paste is formed.
3 Heat the oils in a large heavy-based pan. Add the spice paste and cook over low heat for about 10 minutes, or until it is golden brown in colour with oil forming around the edges. Add a little water if the mixture starts to stick or burn.
4 Add the beef and cook over high heat, stirring, for 5 minutes, until browned. Add the cumin and combine well. Pour in the stock and simmer, covered, for about 2 hours, or until the meat is tender. Add the baby squash for the last 20 minutes of cooking. Remove the lid for the final 10 minutes of cooking until the sauce reduces and thickens. Season with salt to taste and sprinkle with the garlic chives. Serve with steamed rice (if preferred) and accompany with the lemon wedges.

NUTRITION PER SERVE
Protein 40 g; Fat 55 g; Carbohydrate 5 g; Dietary Fibre 2 g; Cholesterol 130 mg; 2735 kJ (655 cal)

Trim the baby green squash with a sharp knife, and cut in half vertically.

Process the onion, spices and oil until a thick paste forms.

Cook the paste until it is golden brown with oil forming around the edges.

Add the baby squash, and cook until the sauce reduces and thickens.

MUSAMAN CURRY

Preparation time: 30 minutes
Total cooking time: 1 hour 20 minutes
Serves 4–6

4 dried red chillies
3 teaspoons ground coriander
3 teaspoons ground cumin
2 teaspoons cinnamon
1 teaspoon nutmeg
1/2 teaspoon ground cloves
1 teaspoon cracked black pepper
1 large onion, chopped
4 cloves garlic, roughly chopped
2 stems lemongrass (white part only), sliced
2 tablespoons oil
800 g (1 lb 10 oz) blade steak, cut into bite-size cubes
2 cups (500 ml/16 fl oz) coconut milk
500 g (1 lb) baby potatoes
250 g (8 oz) baby onions
1 tablespoon tamarind concentrate
3 tablespoons soft brown sugar
1 tablespoon lime juice

1 Place the chillies, coriander, cumin, cinnamon, nutmeg, cloves and pepper in a dry frying pan. Cook over low heat for 4 minutes, shaking the pan regularly until the spices are brown and fragrant. Cool, then place in a food processor with the onion, garlic, lemon grass and about 2 teaspoons of the oil. Process to a smooth paste.

2 Heat the remaining oil in a heavy-based pan and brown the meat in two batches. Add the spice paste and toss to coat the meat. Cook for 2 minutes.

3 Add the coconut milk and simmer for 30 minutes. Add the potatoes and onions and simmer for a further 30 minutes, stirring occasionally, or until the meat and vegetables are tender and the sauce is thick.

4 Add the tamarind, sugar and lime juice. Simmer for a further 3 minutes. Serve with rice.

NUTRITION PER SERVE (6)
Protein 35 g; Fat 30 g; Carbohydrate 25 g; Dietary Fibre 5 g; Cholesterol 70 mg; 2095 kJ (500 cal)

Remove the tough outer layers of the lemon grass and slice the white part.

Cook the spices in a frying pan until they are brown and fragrant.

Add the tamarind, sugar and lime juice to the pan and simmer for 3 minutes.

CHILLI

PERI PERI PRAWNS

Preparation time: 20 minutes
+ 3 hours marinating
Total cooking time: 10 minutes
Serves 4

3 tablespoons sunflower oil
3 tablespoons olive oil
2 teaspoons dried chilli flakes
4 large cloves garlic, crushed
1 teaspoon salt
1 kg (2 lb) raw prawns
75 g (2½ oz) butter
3 tablespoons lemon juice

1 Place the oils, chilli flakes, garlic and salt in a large glass bowl and mix well. Shell and devein the prawns, leaving the tails intact. Place in the chilli mixture and refrigerate for 3 hours, stirring and turning occasionally.

2 Preheat the grill to very hot. Place the prawns in a single layer on a baking tray and brush with any of the remaining oil and chilli mixture. Grill for about 5 minutes, or until tender.

3 Meanwhile, melt the butter with the lemon juice in a small pan and pour into a serving jug. Serve the prawns hot, drizzled with the lemon butter.

NUTRITION PER SERVE
Protein 20 g; Fat 45 g; Carbohydrate 1 g; Dietary Fibre 1 g; Cholesterol 285 mg; 2055 kJ (490 cal)

COOK'S FILE

Note: You can use 1–2 chopped red Bird's Eye chillies instead of flakes.

Mix the oils, chilli, garlic and salt together in a large glass bowl.

Peel and devein the prawns leaving the tails intact.

Brush the prawns with any remaining oil and chilli mixture.

Melt the butter and lemon juice together while the prawns are cooking.

GRILLED SALMON WITH CHILLI-CORN SALSA

Preparation time: 25 minutes
Total cooking time: 15 minutes
Serves 4

1 tablespoon olive oil
1/2 teaspoon ground cumin
1/2 teaspoon paprika
4 salmon cutlets
4 limes, cut into quarters, to serve

Chilli-Corn Salsa
2 corn cobs, husks and threads removed
4 spring onions, finely sliced
1 small clove garlic, crushed
1/2 red capsicum, finely diced
1 teaspoon seeded and finely chopped red jalapeno chilli
1 teaspoon seeded and finely chopped green jalapeno chilli
1 teaspoon ground cumin
2 tablespoons extra virgin olive oil
2 tablespoons lime juice
1 tablespoon finely chopped parsley

1 Combine the olive oil with the cumin and paprika and set aside.

2 To make Chilli-Corn Salsa: Bring a large pan of water to the boil. Add the corn cobs and cook until tender. Drain and plunge into icy cold water to cool. Cut off the kernels and combine in a large bowl with the spring onion, garlic, capsicum, chilli, cumin, extra virgin olive oil, lime juice and parsley. Season to taste with salt and pepper.

3 Brush the salmon with the spicy oil and cook on a hot barbecue grill or in a chargrill pan. Cook for 2 minutes each side for salmon that is still rare on the inside, or leave for a few extra minutes for salmon that is well done. Take care not to overcook. Serve immediately with the Chilli and Corn Salsa and the lime quarters.

NUTRITION PER SERVE
Protein 20 g; Fat 25 g; Carbohydrate 20 g; Dietary Fibre 3 g; Cholesterol 70 mg; 1695 kJ (405 cal)

COOK'S FILE

Note: The Salsa is also delicious served with barbecued meats.

Combine the olive oil with the ground cumin and the paprika.

Slice the kernels from the cooled corn cobs with a sharp knife.

Cook the salmon cutlets for about 2 minutes on each side.

CHILLI TOMATO SOUP

Preparation time: 20 minutes
Total cooking time: 30 minutes
Serves 4

1 kg (2 lb) ripe tomatoes
25 g (3/4 oz) butter
1 small onion, finely chopped
4 anchovy fillets, drained
2 Bird's Eye chillies, seeded and finely chopped
1 strip lemon rind, pith removed
2 cups (500 ml/16 fl oz) chicken stock
1 bay leaf
1–2 teaspoons sugar
sour cream and 2 tablespoons fresh coriander leaves, to serve

1 Score a cross in the base of each tomato and plunge into boiling water for 10 seconds. Place in cold water and then peel the skin away from the cross and roughly chop. If very ripe tomatoes are unavailable, use canned.
2 Heat the butter in a large pan, add the onion and cook over medium heat until softened. Add the anchovies and cook for 1 minute, breaking up the fish with a wooden spoon. Add the tomato, chilli, lemon rind, stock and bay leaf. Bring to the boil, then reduce the heat and simmer for 20 minutes. Add sugar, to taste, and season with salt and freshly ground black pepper.
3 Remove the lemon rind and bay leaf. Cool the soup slightly, and process in batches in a food processor or blender until smooth. Reheat and serve with a swirl of sour cream, and scattered with coriander leaves.

NUTRITION PER SERVE
Protein 5 g; Fat 15 g; Carbohydrate 10 g; Dietary Fibre 4 g; Cholesterol 45 mg; 765 kJ (180 cal)

Peel away the skin from the tomatoes before roughly chopping.

Add the tomato, chilli, lemon rind, stock and bay leaf to the pan.

Process the soup in batches, to prevent overflowing.

CHICKEN QUESADILLAS

Preparation time: 45 minutes
+ 1 hour marinating
Total cooking time: 20–30 minutes
Serves 4

4 large green chillies
3 large red chillies
2 chicken breast fillets
3 tablespoons wholegrain mustard
2 tablespoons honey
4 flour tortillas
3 cups (375 g/12 oz) grated Cheddar
6 spring onions,finely sliced
1–2 small red chillies, finely sliced (optional)
1–2 small green chillies, finely sliced (optional)
oilve oil, for cooking

Green Chilli Salsa
3 long green chillies, finely sliced
2 tomatoes, peeled, seeded and chopped
1 onion, finely chopped
1/3 cup (15 g/1/2 oz) fresh coriander leaves, finely chopped
2 tablespoons freshly squeezed lime juice

1 Place the large chillies under a hot grill and cook for 5–8 minutes, turning frequently, until the skins are blackened. Place them in a plastic bag and leave to cool. Remove the skin and seeds. Cut them in half, then slice the flesh into fine strips.

2 Place the chicken in a deep dish. Combine the mustard and honey and add to the chicken. Turn the meat until well coated with the mixture. Cover and refrigerate for 1 hour. Place the chicken under a hot grill and cook for 4 minutes each side, or until tender. Cool slightly, then cut into fine strips. Arrange all the remaining ingredients on the bench, ready to assemble the quesadillas.

3 To make Green Chilli Salsa: Combine all the salsa ingredients in a bowl and mix well, adding a little more lime juice if desired. Set aside to allow the flavours to combine.

4 Lightly grease a large, heavy-based frying pan and warm over medium heat. Place one tortilla in the pan and sprinkle with a quarter of the Cheddar and half the spring onion, roasted chilli, chicken and sliced chilli. Sprinkle with a third of the remaining Cheddar and top with another tortilla.

5 Brush lightly with a little oil, invert the quesadilla onto a plate and then slide back into the pan so the top becomes the bottom. Cook for a few minutes longer, just until the Cheddar has melted and the underside looks golden and crisp. Slide the quesadilla onto a plate and keep warm.

6 Repeat with another tortilla, adding half of the remaining Cheddar, the remaining spring onion, roasted chilli, chicken, and sliced chilli. Top with the rest of the Cheddar and the last tortilla. Serve immediately, cut into halves or triangles, with the Salsa.

NUTRITION PER SERVE
Protein 45 g; Fat 35 g; Carbohydrate 40 g; Dietary Fibre 5 g; Cholesterol 125 mg; 2665 kJ (635 cal)

COOK'S FILE

Note: Flour tortillas are available from most supermarkets, in the bread section—they may need trimming slightly to fit in the frying pan.

Remove the blackened skins from the grilled chillies.

Turn the chicken to coat well with the mustard mixture.

Combine all the salsa ingredients in a bowl and mix well.

Sprinkle the tortilla with one-quarter of the grated Cheddar.

Cover the Cheddar, chicken, chilli and spring onion filling with another tortilla.

Invert the quesadilla onto a plate, then slide it back into the pan.

GRILLED VEGETABLES WITH WARM CHILLI DRESSING

Preparation time: 15 minutes
Total cooking time: 20 minutes
Serves 4 as a starter

- 1 red capsicum, seeded and cut into strips
- 1 green capsicum, seeded and cut into strips
- 2 zucchini, cut into thin strips lengthways
- 1 eggplant (about 150 g/4¾ oz), cut into 8 slices
- 2 tomatoes, each cut into 3 thick slices horizontally
- olive oil, for brushing

Dressing
- 3 tablespoons extra virgin olive oil
- 2 cloves garlic, finely chopped
- 1 tablespoon finely chopped and seeded jalapeno chilli
- ¼ teaspoon hot dried chilli flakes
- 1 teaspoon sugar
- 2 tablespoons lemon juice
- 1 tablespoon chopped parsley
- ¼ teaspoon salt

1 Preheat the grill to very hot. (You can use a barbecue or heavy-ridged grill pan, if preferred.) Brush the vegetables with olive oil. Grill each type of vegetable separately until softened but with a 'bite'. Arrange the vegetables on a serving platter.

2 To make Dressing: Heat the extra virgin olive oil in a small pan with the garlic, jalapeno and dried chilli. Cook over very low heat until the garlic and jalapeno has softened. Add the sugar and lemon juice and heat gently. Stir in the parsley and salt and drizzle over the vegetables. Sprinkle with lots of cracked black pepper and serve.

NUTRITION PER SERVE
Protein 5 g; Fat 15 g; Carbohydrate 10 g; Dietary Fibre 5 g; Cholesterol 0 mg; 770 kJ (185 cal)

Prepare the vegetables, cutting the zucchini lengthways into thin strips.

Cook the garlic and fresh and dried chilli over low heat until softened.

Add the parsley and salt to the Dressing and stir well to combine.

CHILLI CON CARNE

Preparation time: 10 minutes
Total cooking time: 50 minutes
Serves 4

1 tablespoon olive oil
1 onion, chopped
3 cloves garlic, crushed
1 stick celery, chopped
500 g (1 lb) lean minced beef
2 teaspoons chilli powder
pinch of cayenne pepper
1 teaspoon dried oregano
440 g (14 oz) can crushed tomatoes
2 tablespoons tomato paste
1 teaspoon soft brown sugar
1 tablespoon cider or red wine vinegar
425 g (13½ oz) can red kidney beans, rinsed and drained

1 Heat the oil in a large, heavy-based pan and add the onion, garlic and celery. Stir over medium heat for 5 minutes, or until softened. Add the beef and cook over high heat for 5 minutes until well browned, breaking up any lumps with a fork.

2 Add the chilli powder, cayenne pepper and oregano to the pan. Cook for a further 2 minutes. Add the crushed tomatoes, ½ cup (125 ml/4 fl oz) water and the tomato paste and stir to combine.

3 Simmer for 30 minutes, stirring occasionally. Add the sugar, cider vinegar or red wine vinegar, the kidney beans and season with salt and freshly ground black pepper. Heat through for 5 minutes.

NUTRITION PER SERVE
Protein 40 g; Fat 20 g; Carbohydrate 20 g; Dietary Fibre 15 g; Cholesterol 80 mg; 1775 kJ (425 cal)

COOK'S FILE

Note: For the best flavour, make this dish a day in advance if possible.

Cook the meat, breaking up any lumps of meat with a fork.

Add the crushed tomatoes, water and tomato paste to the pan.

Add the kidney beans and heat through for 5 minutes.

Chilli Varieties

Identifying and naming chillies correctly is a difficult task. Names vary from country to country and growers seem to make up new ones all the time. Here we describe a few of the varieties available nowadays, as well as powders and sauces which can add fire to your cooking.

The availability of specific types of chilli is often limited, so most of our recipes just call for a quantity of red or green chillies. (Always use fresh unless otherwise stated.) Use whatever you can find, but do experiment with different types when available. Red chillies are simply ripened green chillies and are a little sweeter, just like the difference between a red and a green capsicum.

FRESH CHILLIES

Banana chilli

Also called a Hungarian sweet chilli, Banana chillies can be red, green or yellow. They are large, low in heat and thick fleshed, and are often served stuffed or roasted.

Bird's Eye

This is a small, very hot chilli. Both red and green types are available. They are commonly used in Asian cooking.

Habanero (*hab-an-yero*)

Said to be the hottest of all chillies, the habanero changes from green to orange to red, and can be used at any of these stages. It is one for the true chilli fanatic.

Hungarian Cherry Peppers

These are small, round, red or green chillies with a medium heat. They are slightly sweet and are ideal for salads and pickles.

Inca Gold

Also known as Aji Amarillo, this orange chilli has quite a distinctive, fruity flavour and is extremely hot. It can be used for stuffing and baking, or finely chopped in salsas and fish dishes.

Inferno

This is a thin yellowish-green chilli. As the name implies, it is very hot.

Jalapeno (*hal-ap-enyo*)

This chilli is smooth, thick-fleshed and medium in heat. It is available in either red or green. The skin sometimes has fine brown lines like cracks running along it. This is a characteristic of jalapenos.

Jamaican bell

This extremely hot chilli is related to the habanero and Scotch bonnet. It is small, red and thin-fleshed. It is used in salsas, chutneys and curries, and goes particularly well with tropical fruits.

Large or long chillies

These may be labelled Dutch or Korean in the shops. Use them wherever large or long chillies are called for.

Poblano

This is a large, mild to hot chilli which has a fairly thick flesh and a subtle smoky flavour. They are usually roasted and stuffed, rather than chopped and added to dishes. When dried they are known as Ancho chillies.

Scotch bonnet

Scotch bonnets can be yellow, orange or red with a fiery, fruity, smoky flavour. Scotch bonnets are a key ingredient in Caribbean cooking and condiment sauces. To retain the flavour, but reduce the heat, the chillies can be added whole to the pan while cooking and then removed just before serving.

Serrano

Commonly used after they have matured to red, these chillies have a moderate heat and a smooth skin.

Thai

These are long, thin, pointed chillies, which have a lingering heat. Both red and green types are available. As they are thin-fleshed and difficult to skin and seed, it is better to use them whole. Thai chillies are used extensively in Southeast Asian cooking.

DRIED CHILLIES

Soak these chillies in boiling water for a few minutes to rehydrate them before use.

Ancho

This deep reddish-mahogany chilli is the most common of the Mexican dried varieties. It has a sweet, fruity flavour with a hint of plum and a mild heat. It is available from most speciality food stores.

Cascabel

Named after the rattling sound it makes, this round, dark, reddish-brown chilli is medium-hot and releases a smoky, woody, nutty flavour in sauces and salsas.

Chipotle (*chi-poht-lay*)

This is a jalapeno chilli which has been dried and smoked. The process produces a brittle chilli with a strong woody, smoky flavour. They are available from speciality food stores, either dried in packets or canned in adobo sauce.

Common dried red chillies

The size and degree of heat of these chillies will vary, depending on which type has been dried (it is not usually specified). They are a typical ingredient of Southeast Asian cooking.

New Mexico

Dark red in colour, these chillies have an earthy, fruity flavour and give a medium heat to food. Due to their wonderful flavour, it is better to use them in cooking without too many additional herbs and spices. Most speciality food stores should have them in stock.

SPICES AND CONDIMENTS

Adobo sauce

This reddish-brown piquant Mexican sauce is made from ancho chillies, vinegar, tomato paste and herbs. It has a smoky chocolate flavour. Use it as a marinade or as a serving sauce for meats and vegetables.

Cayenne pepper

This consists of dried Cayenne chillies that have been finely ground. The pepper is very hot.

Chilli paste jam

This is a tangy, sweet chilli paste sold in jars at Asian food stores. It is used in stir-fry sauces and some soups. After opening, store it in the refrigerator.

Chilli powder

Dried red chillies are finely ground to make this powder. The containers are marked as either 'hot' or 'mild', but the heat will differ between manufacturers.

Dried chilli flakes

These are dried and coarsely crushed chillies. Add the flakes during cooking or place on the table as a condiment.

Paprika

This powder is made from finely ground, dried pimento. It can often be marked 'sweet' or 'hot', and is commonly used in Eastern European cooking.

Piri Piri Sauce

This is a Portuguese Chilli sauce made from chillies, garlic, ginger, spices and oil. The Portuguese use it to baste Charcoal Chicken, but it can also be used as a serving sauce with other meats, fish and seafood.

Sambal oelek

Chillies, vinegar, sugar and salt are used to make this spicy, hot purée, which is used in Asian food or as a condiment.

Sweet chilli sauce

This is a sweet, hot, syrupy sauce used widely in Thai cookery. Add it to dishes during cooking, or serve at the table as a condiment or dipping sauce. It is available, bottled, in most supermarkets.

Tabasco sauce

Made in Louisiana from Tabasco chillies, salt and vinegar, and aged in oak barrels, Tabasco sauce can be added to dishes at any stage of cooking to add a little (or a lot) of zing. Alternatively use it as a condiment at the table.

BOTTLED AND CANNED CHILLIES

Although bottled and canned chillies tend to lose their crispy texture and intensity of flavour during processing, they are a convenient substitute when fresh or dried chillies are unavailable.

Chipotles adobado

Commonly canned with an adobo sauce, chipotles retain their smoky flavour and heat. They can be stored in a glass or plastic container in the refrigerator for 1 month.

Pickled jalapenos

Usually available in bottled form, pickled jalapenos are a pale yellow–green colour and retain their crunchy texture. They have a tangy, vinegar flavour. Once opened, store in the refrigerator for up to 1 month.

BALINESE CHILLI SQUID

Preparation time: 30 minutes
Total cooking time: 10 minutes
Serves 4

750 g (1½ lb) squid hoods
¼ cup (60 ml/2 fl oz) lime juice
2 tablespoons vegetable oil
1 large red chilli, seeded and sliced
3 spring onions, sliced
1 tablespoon vegetable oil, extra
1 tablespoon tamarind concentrate
1 stem lemon grass, white part only, finely sliced
1 cup (250 ml/8 fl oz) chicken stock
5 Thai basil leaves, shredded

Spice Paste
2 large red chillies, seeded and chopped
2 cloves garlic, chopped
2 cm (¾ inch) piece fresh ginger, chopped
2 cm (¾ inch) piece fresh turmeric, chopped
3 spring onions, chopped
1 tomato, peeled, seeded and chopped
2 teaspoons coriander seeds
1 teaspoon dried shrimp paste

1 Cut the squid into large pieces and score the tender flesh. Place in a bowl, with the lime juice and season well.
2 To make Spice Paste: Grind the chilli, garlic, ginger, turmeric, spring onion, tomato, coriander and shrimp paste in a food processor.
3 Heat the oil in a wok. Cook the squid, chilli and spring onion in batches for 2 minutes over medium heat. Remove from the wok.
4 Heat the extra oil and add Spice Paste, tamarind concentrate and lemon grass. Cook, stirring, over medium heat for 5 minutes.
5 Return the squid to the wok and add the stock. Season with pepper and add the basil. Bring to the boil, then reduce the heat and simmer for 2 minutes.

NUTRITION PER SERVE
Protein 35 g; Fat 15 g; Carbohydrate 3 g; Dietary Fibre 2 g; Cholesterol 375 mg; 1245 kJ (295 cal)

Seed and slice 2 fresh red chillies with sharp knife.

Cut the squid into large pieces and score the tender flesh.

After adding the lime juice, season the squid pieces well with salt and pepper.

Cook the squid in batches for 2 minutes over moderate heat.

Grind the spices for the Chilli Paste in a mortar and pestle.

Add the chicken and soy sauce to the pan and stir in.

Fry 100 g (3⅓ oz) of the noodles in hot oil until crisp. Drain on paper towels.

Cook the remaining noodles in boiling water until just tender.

COCONUT CHICKEN SOUP

Preparation time: 20 minutes
Total cooking time: 25 minutes
Serves 4

Chilli Paste
4 dried chillies, roughly chopped
1 teaspoon coriander seeds
1 teaspoon grated fresh ginger
1 spring onion, chopped
½ teaspoon ground turmeric

3 cups (750 ml/24 fl oz) coconut milk
350 g (11¼ oz) chicken breast fillets, thinly sliced
2 tablespoons light soy sauce
2 cups (500 ml/16 fl oz) chicken stock
400 g (12⅔ oz) dried egg noodles
peanut oil, for deep-frying
spring onion and red chillies, to serve

1 To make Chilli Paste: Stir the ingredients in a small pan over low heat for 5 minutes until fragrant. Transfer to a mortar and pestle or food processor and grind until smooth.

2 Heat 1 cup (250 ml/8 fl oz) of the coconut milk in a pan; add the Chilli Paste and stir for 2–3 minutes. Add the chicken and soy sauce and cook for 3–4 minutes. Stir in the remaining coconut milk and stock. Bring to the boil, then simmer for 10 minutes.

3 Break 100 g (3⅓ oz) of the noodles into large pieces. Fry in hot peanut oil until crisp; drain on paper towels. Cook the remaining noodles in boiling water until just tender and drain.

4 Place the boiled noodles in serving bowls and ladle the soup over the top. Garnish with fried noodles and serve with sliced spring onion and chillies.

NUTRITION PER SERVE
Protein 35 g; Fat 35 g; Carbohydrate 75 g; Dietary Fibre 3 g; Cholesterol 60 mg; 2025 kJ (480 cal)

FISH WRAPPED IN BANANA LEAVES

Preparation time: 20 minutes
Total cooking time: 35 minutes
Serves 4–6

Spice Paste

1 red onion, finely chopped
3 small red chillies, seeded and chopped
1 teaspoon dried shrimp paste
1 cm (1/2 inch) piece fresh galangal, finely chopped
1 stem lemon grass, white part only, finely sliced
5 blanched almonds, chopped
2 tablespoons water
4 kaffir lime leaves, finely shredded

2 teaspoons sesame oil
1 tablespoon vegetable oil
1 teaspoon soy sauce
1 banana leaf, (about 50 cm x 30 cm/20 x 12 inches)
1 whole trout or silver bream (about 750 g/ 1 1/2 lb), cleaned and scaled

1 To make Spice Paste: Grind all the ingredients except the kaffir lime leaves in a food processor until smooth. Transfer to a bowl and mix in the kaffir lime leaves. Set aside.

2 Preheat the oven to moderate 180°C (350°F/Gas 4). Heat the sesame oil and vegetable oil in a small frying pan and gently fry the Spice Paste for 5 minutes. Mix in the soy sauce. Remove from the heat and cool.

3 Cut a large rectangle from the banana leaf and brush with oil. Wash the fish well under running water and pat dry. Score the fish several times on both sides and rub in the Spice Paste, pushing it well into the slits.

4 Place the fish on the banana leaf and fold over to make a parcel. Wrap again in foil to secure. Bake for 25–30 minutes, or until the flesh flakes easily when tested with a fork. Unwrap the fish and serve garnished with shredded lime leaves and sliced orange chillies, if desired.

NUTRITION PER SERVE (6)
Protein 30 g; Fat 15 g; Carbohydrate 3 g; Dietary Fibre 1 g; Cholesterol 75 mg; 1050 kJ (250 cal)

Add the shredded kaffir lime leaves to the Spice Paste.

Stir the soy sauce into the fried Spice Paste and mix well.

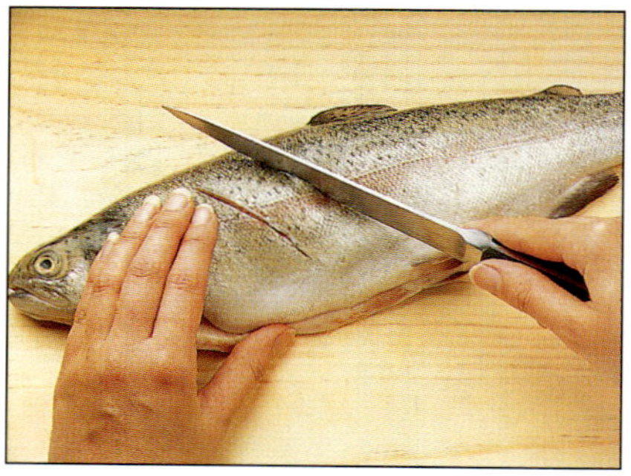

Score the fish several times on both sides with a sharp knife.

Wrap the fish in the banana leaf, folding the ends securely.

WATERMELON AND PINEAPPLE SALAD WITH JALAPENO SYRUP

Preparation time: 15 minutes
Total cooking time: 20 minutes
Serves 4

Jalapeno Syrup
1/2 cup (125 ml/4 fl oz) fresh lime juice
1/2 cup (125 g/4 oz) sugar

2 jalapeno chillies, stemmed and sliced into thin rounds

1/2 small round watermelon, cut into small cubes
1 small ripe pineapple, peeled and cut into small triangles
fresh mint sprigs, to serve

1 **To make the Jalapeno Syrup:** Stir the lime juice, sugar and 1/2 cup (125 ml/4 fl oz) water in a small pan over medium-low heat without boiling until the sugar has completely dissolved. Bring to the boil, then simmer for 10–15 minutes, without stirring, or until thick and syrupy.
2 Add the chilli; cook for 5 minutes. Allow to cool to room temperature.
3 Arrange the fruit on a plate; drizzle with the Syrup. Garnish with the mint and extra chilli slices. Serve chilled.

NUTRITION PER SERVE
Protein 2 g; Fat 0 g; Carbohydrate 45 g; Dietary Fibre 3 g; Cholesterol 0 mg; 745 kJ (180 cal)

Peel and slice the pineapple and cut the slices into small triangles.

Simmer the syrup, without boiling, until all the sugar has dissolved.

Add the sliced Jalapeno chilli to the syrup and cook for 5 minutes.

SKEWERED LAMB WITH CHILLI AIOLI

Preparation time: 20–25 minutes
+ overnight marinating
Total cooking time: 15 minutes
Makes 12 skewers

1.5 kg (3 lb) leg of lamb, boned
1/2 cup (125 ml/4 fl oz) olive oil
1/2 cup (125 ml/4 fl oz) lemon juice
2 cloves garlic, crushed
1 teaspoon cracked black pepper
1 tablespoon Dijon mustard
1 tablespoon chopped oregano

Chilli Aioli
2–3 small red chillies, seeds and stem removed
3 cloves garlic, peeled
1/2 teaspoon freshly ground black pepper
3 egg yolks
2 tablespoons lemon juice
200 ml (6 1/2 fl oz) olive oil

1 Cut the lamb into cubes; place in a large bowl. Add the combined olive oil, lemon juice, garlic, pepper, mustard and oregano and mix well. Cover; refrigerate several hours or overnight.

2 Drain the lamb, reserving the marinade. Thread the lamb onto the skewers. Grill under a hot, preheated grill until well browned, brushing with the marinade occasionally.

3 To make Chilli Aioli: In a food processor, chop the chillies and garlic for 30 seconds. Add the black pepper, egg yolks and 2 teaspoons of lemon juice. With the motor running, slowly pour in the oil in a fine stream. Increase the flow as the Aioli thickens. Add the remaining lemon juice and season to taste. Serve with the skewered lamb.

NUTRITION PER SKEWER
Protein 20 g; Fat 15 g; Carbohydrate 0 g; Dietary Fibre 0 g; Cholesterol 55 mg; 810 kJ (190 cal)

Mix the lamb pieces with the marinade to thoroughly coat the meat.

Thread 4 pieces of marinated lamb onto each skewer.

Pour the oil in a fine stream into the food processor.

PRAWN, PAWPAW AND CHILLI SALAD

Preparation time: 35 minutes
Total cooking time: Nil
Serves 4

3 tablespoons olive oil
3 tablespoons lime juice
1 tablespoon fish sauce
2 teaspoons grated palm sugar
1 teaspoon seeded, finely chopped red jalapeno chilli
1 teaspoon seeded, finely chopped green jalapeno chilli
800 g (1 lb 10 oz) cooked king prawns
400 g (12 2/3 oz) pawpaw
1 small red onion, finely sliced
2 tablespoons shredded mint
2 tablespoons finely chopped fresh coriander

1 Combine the olive oil, lime juice, fish sauce, palm sugar and chilli in a large mixing bowl and set aside to allow the flavours to combine.

2 Meanwhile, peel and devein the prawns, leaving the tails intact. Peel and discard the seeds from the pawpaw, and cut into bite-size pieces.

3 Add the prawns, pawpaw, onion mint and coriander to the bowl. Very gently, using 2 spoons, toss the salad to combine. Add the chilli dressing and toss gently again to coat just before serving.

NUTRITION PER SERVE
Protein 25 g; Fat 15 g; Carbohydrate 10 g; Dietary Fibre 3 g; Cholesterol 190 mg; 1175 kJ (280 cal)

COOK'S FILE

Note: Palm sugar is a very dark brown sugar used in Asian cooking. If it is not available, use soft brown sugar instead.

Combine the oil, juice, fish sauce, palm sugar and chillies in a large mixing bowl.

Peel and devein the prawns with your fingers, leaving the tails intact.

Gently toss the mixture to combine all the ingredients, using 2 spoons.

CHILLI BEEF WITH SPINACH

Preparation time: 30 minutes
+ 20 minutes marinating
Total cooking time: 15 minutes
Serves 3–4

500 g (1 lb) rump or fillet steak
2 tablespoons rice wine
1 tablespoon cornflour
4 tablespoons soy sauce
3 tablespoons peanut oil
250 g (8 oz) baby Chinese spinach with pink roots
2 tablespoons salted black beans
2 teaspoons finely chopped fresh ginger
2 cloves garlic, finely chopped
1 long green chilli, seeded and cut into fine strips
1 long red chilli, seeded and cut into fine strips
1 tablespoon sesame oil
1 teaspoon sugar
2 teaspoons peanut oil, extra
4 cloves garlic, finely sliced

1 Trim the meat of any excess fat and sinew and slice across the grain into thin strips. Combine the rice wine, cornflour and 2 tablespoons of the soy sauce in a bowl. Stir in 1 tablespoon of the peanut oil. Add the beef and mix well to coat. Cover and leave to marinate in the refrigerator for 20 minutes.

2 Wash and dry the spinach. Leave the pink roots on, but trim away the straggly ends. Cut the leaves from the stems, as these will need less cooking. Rinse the black beans under cold running water, then drain and mash with the back of a spoon.

3 Drain the meat and discard the marinade. Heat 1 tablespoon of the peanut oil in a wok or large frying pan, and cook the meat quickly over high heat, in two batches, until just browned. Do not overcook. Remove from the wok and set aside.

4 Heat the remaining peanut oil in the wok and stir-fry the ginger, garlic chilli and black beans for 1–2 minutes. Return the beef to the pan with the sesame oil, sugar and remaining soy sauce. Stir-fry briefly until the beef is heated through. Remove from the wok, cover and set aside. Keep warm.

5 Working quickly, wipe out the wok with paper towels and heat the extra peanut oil. Add the sliced garlic and cook for about 30 seconds, until lightly golden.

6 Add the spinach stems and 1 tablespoon of water. Stir-fry for 30 seconds, until the spinach is bright green. Add the spinach leaves and toss until just wilted. Serve immediately with the beef.

NUTRITION PER SERVE (4)
Protein 35 g; Fat 25 g; Carbohydrate 5 g; Dietary Fibre 3 g; Cholesterol 85 mg; 1615 kJ (385 cal)

COOK'S FILE

Note: If Chinese spinach is unavailable, use baby English spinach instead. Salted black beans are available from Asian speciality shops. They will keep, refrigerated, in an airtight container, for up to 12 months.

Hint: To make the beef easier to slice, freeze it until it is just firm, and thinly slice while it is still frozen.

Variation: Pork fillet is a great substitute for the beef. Trim any excess fat and sinew and cut across the grain into thin round slices.

Add the beef to the marinade and mix well to coat.

Wash and dry the spinach, then trim away the scraggly end of the roots.

Rinse the black beans under cold running water, then drain.

Stir-fry the beef in batches to prevent overcrowding the pan.

Stir-fry the ginger, garlic, chilli and black beans until fragrant.

Add the spinach leaves to the pan and toss until wilted.

THREE BEAN CHILLI

Preparation time: 20 minutes
+ 2 hours standing
Total cooking time: 1 hour 35 minutes
Serves 4

1 cup (220 g/7 oz) dried black beans (see note)
2 tablespoons oil
1 large onion, finely chopped
3 cloves garlic, crushed
2 tablespoons ground cumin
1 tablespoon ground coriander
1 teaspoon ground cinnamon
1 teaspoon chilli powder
400 g (12 2/3 oz) can crushed tomatoes
1 1/2 cups (375 ml/12 fl oz) vegetable stock
400 g (12 2/3 oz) can chickpeas, rinsed and drained
400 g (12 2/3 oz) can red kidney beans, rinsed and drained
2 tablespoons tomato paste
1 tablespoon sugar
sour cream and corn chips, to serve

1 Place the black beans in a large pan, cover with water and bring to the boil. Turn off the heat and set aside for 2 hours. Drain the beans, cover with fresh water and boil for 1 hour, until the beans are tender but not mushy. Drain well.
2 Heat the oil in a large pan and cook the onion over medium-low heat for 5 minutes, until golden, stirring frequently. Reduce the heat, add the garlic and spices; stir for 1 minute.
3 Add the tomatoes, stock, chickpeas, kidney beans and black beans and combine with the onion mixture. Bring to the boil, then simmer for 20 minutes, stirring occasionally.
4 Add the tomato paste, sugar and salt and pepper, to taste. Simmer for a further 5 minutes. Serve with sour cream and corn chips on the side.

NUTRITION PER SERVE
Protein 40 g; Fat 55 g; Carbohydrate 125 g; Dietary Fibre 36 g; Cholesterol 40 mg; 4775 kJ (1140 cal)

COOK'S FILE

Note: If black beans are unavailable, double the quantity of kidney beans and chickpeas.

Do not confuse black beans with Asian black beans, which are fermented soy.

Cook the chopped onion, stirring frequently, until it turns golden.

Add the tomatoes, stock, chickpeas, kidney beans and black beans to the pan.

Add salt and pepper to taste and simmer for a further 5 minutes.

FRIED CLAMS IN ROASTED CHILLI PASTE

Preparation time: 15 minutes
Total cooking time: 12–15 minutes
Serves 4

Roasted Chilli Paste

2 tablespoons vegetable oil
2 spring onions, sliced
2 cloves garlic, sliced
1/4 cup (85 g/2 3/4 oz) small dried shrimps
6 small red chillies, seeded
2 teaspoons palm sugar
2 teaspoons fish sauce
2 teaspoons tamarind concentrate
pinch of salt

3 cloves garlic, finely sliced
3 small red chillies, seeded and sliced lengthways
1 tablespoon light soy sauce
1 cup (250 ml/8 fl oz) chicken stock
1 kg (2 lb) clams, scrubbed
1/2 cup (25 g/3/4 oz) Thai basil leaves
steamed Jasmine rice, to serve

1 To make Roasted Chilli Paste: Heat the oil in a wok and fry the spring onion, garlic, dried shrimps and chillies until golden brown. Remove from the pan with a slotted spoon and reserve the oil.

2 Place the onion, garlic, shrimps, chillies and sugar in a mortar and pestle or small food processor and grind until the mixture is well blended. Add the fish sauce, tamarind concentrate and salt. Blend or grind to obtain a finely textured paste. Transfer to a bowl and set aside.

3 Heat the reserved oil in a wok. Add the garlic, chilli, Roasted Chilli Paste and soy sauce. Mix well, then add the chicken stock and bring just to the boil. Add the clams and cook over medium-high heat for 2–3 minutes. Discard any unopened clams. Stir in the basil and serve immediately with steamed Jasmine rice.

NUTRITION PER SERVE
Protein 30 g; Fat 15 g; Carbohydrate 90 g; Dietary Fibre 5 g; Cholesterol 280 mg; 2490 kJ (700 cal)

Use a slotted spoon to remove the onion, garlic, shrimps and chillies from the wok.

Blend or grind the mixture to obtain a finely textured paste.

Remove any clams that have not opened from the wok.

BLACK BEAN SCALLOPS IN GINGER CHILLI OIL

Preparation time: 10–15 minutes
Total cooking time: 8 minutes
Serves 4

Ginger Chilli Oil

1/3 cup (80 ml/2 3/4 fl oz) peanut oil
3 dried red chillies, crushed
2 cm (3/4 inch) piece fresh ginger, grated
1 clove garlic, thinly sliced
1 tablespoon sesame oil
1 tablespoon soy sauce

2 tablespoons peanut oil
3 cm (1 1/4 inch) piece fresh ginger, cut into paper thin strips
1 kg (2 lb) scallops, cleaned
2 tablespoons salted black beans, rinsed well
1/4 cup (60 ml/2 fl oz) dry sherry
1 red capsicum, cut into strips
80 g (2 2/3 oz) fresh baby English spinach leaves

1 To make Ginger Chilli Oil: Heat the peanut oil, chilli, ginger and garlic in a pan over medium heat, stirring constantly, for 2 minutes, or until the mixture begins to sizzle. Add the sesame oil and soy sauce and cook for 2 minutes. Remove from the heat; cool slightly; strain and set aside.

2 Heat the peanut oil in a wok or large frying pan over very high heat. Add the ginger; stir for a few seconds then cook the scallops in small batches, tossing frequently.

3 Stir-fry the black beans, sherry and capsicum for 1–2 minutes, then return the scallops to the pan to warm through. Remove from the heat and arrange the scallops on top of the spinach leaves. Drizzle with Ginger Chilli Oil. Serve immediately.

NUTRITION PER SERVE
Protein 35 g; Fat 35 g; Carbohydrate 5 g; Dietary Fibre 5 g; Cholesterol 80 mg; 2035 kJ (485 cal)

Allow the oil to cool slightly, strain into a bowl and set aside.

Cook the scallops in batches over a high heat, tossing them frequently.

Stir-fry the black beans, sherry and capsicum together for 1–2 minutes.

Add the chilli, saffron, cumin, caraway, and salt and pepper to the pan.

Remove the excess oil from the liquid with a spoon.

Add the pumpkin chunks to the pan and cook for 10–15 minutes.

When the beef stock is boiling, add the couscous to the pan.

SPICED LAMB SHANKS WITH COUSCOUS

Preparation time: 30 minutes
Total cooking time: 2 hours 25 minutes
Serves 4

2 tablespoons olive oil
2 tablespoons butter
2 large onions, chopped
3 cloves garlic, finely chopped
5 cm (2 inch) piece fresh ginger, finely chopped
3 fresh red chillies, seeded and finely sliced
1/2 teaspoon saffron threads
1 tablespoon ground cumin
1 teaspoon ground caraway seeds
8 lamb shanks, trimmed and jointed (ask your butcher to joint the lamb for you)
2 cups (500 ml/16 fl oz) beef stock
500 g (1 lb) tomato pasta sauce
300 g (9 2/3 oz) pumpkin, cut into chunks
300 g (9 2/3 oz) yellow squash, halved
300 g (9 2/3 oz) zucchini, cut into large pieces
2 cups (500 ml/16 fl oz) beef stock, extra
2 cups (370 g/11 3/4 oz) couscous

1 Heat the oil and butter in a heavy-based pan. Add the onion, garlic and ginger and cook over low heat until soft and golden. Add the chilli, saffron, cumin, caraway, and salt and pepper, to taste. Cook for 2–3 minutes.

2 Add the lamb; stir to coat the meat. Add the stock and tomato sauce. Bring to the boil, then simmer, covered, for 1 1/2–2 hours, or until the lamb is tender. Skim off any oil.

3 Add the pumpkin and cook for 10–15 minutes. Add the squash and zucchini; cook for a further 10 minutes.

4 Heat the stock in a medium pan until boiling. Add the couscous. Cover tightly and set aside for 3–5 minutes. Fluff up the grains with a fork. Serve with the lamb.

NUTRITION PER SERVE
Protein 75 g; Fat 25 g; Carbohydrate 75 g; Dietary Fibre 10 g; Cholesterol 190 mg; 3385 kJ (810 cal)

CHILLI PRAWN AND CORN CAKES WITH LIME MAYONNAISE

Preparation time: 40 minutes + 2 hours refrigeration
Total cooking time: 10 minutes
Serves 4–6

1 tablespoon light olive oil
2 jalapeno chillies, seeded and finely chopped
1 teaspoon ground coriander
4 spring onions, finely chopped
1/3 cup (20 g/2/3 oz) chopped fresh coriander
500 g (1 lb) cooked prawns, shelled, deveined and finely chopped
130 g (4 1/4 oz) can corn kernels, drained
130 g (4 1/4 oz) can creamed corn
1 egg, lightly beaten
1/3 cup (90 g/3 oz) sour cream
2 1/2 cups (200 g/6 1/2 oz) fresh breadcrumbs
oil, for frying

Lime Mayonnaise
2 egg yolks
1 clove garlic, crushed
1/3 cup (80 ml/2 3/4 fl oz) vegetable oil
1/3 cup (80 ml/2 3/4 fl oz) olive oil
2 tablespoons fresh lime juice
1 small green chilli, finely chopped

1 Heat the olive oil in a pan over medium heat. Add the chilli, ground coriander and spring onion. Fry for 2–3 minutes, stirring constantly.

2 Remove the pan from the heat and add the fresh coriander, prawns, corn kernels and creamed corn. Mix well.

3 Transfer the mixture to a large bowl. Add the egg, sour cream and 1 cup (80 g/2 2/3 oz) of the breadcrumbs. Combine thoroughly and season with salt and pepper, to taste. Cover and refrigerate for 1 1/2–2 hours.

4 Remove the corn mixture from the refrigerator and, using about 1/4 cup of mixture, shape into small patties. Coat all the sides with the remaining breadcrumbs and return to the refrigerator for 30 minutes.

5 Heat the oil in a large frying pan and shallow-fry the Chilli Prawn and Corn Cakes for 3–4 minutes each side, or until golden brown. Remove and drain on paper towels.

6 To make Lime Mayonnaise: Place the egg yolks and garlic in a small bowl. Slowly add the vegetable oil, drop by drop, whisking continuously to form a smooth paste. When all the vegetable oil has been added, slowly add the olive oil in a thin stream while continuing to whisk. Add the lime juice and chilli and mix well. Season to taste with salt and pepper and store in the refrigerator, covered, until needed. Serve with the Chilli Prawn and Corn Cakes.

NUTRITION PER SERVE (6)
Protein 30 g; Fat 40 g; Carbohydrate 30 g; Dietary Fibre 5 g; Cholesterol 265 mg; 2575 kJ (615 cal)

COOK'S FILE

Hint: The corn cake mixture is very soft and needs gentle handling. To make the cakes a little firmer, place in the freezer for 30 minutes.

Note: If you are short on time for making your own Lime Mayonnaise, you can buy a whole egg mayonnaise from the supermarket instead and just add some grated lime rind, chopped chilli and garlic.

Fry the jalapeno chilli, ground coriander and chopped spring onion.

Add the fresh coriander, prawns, corn kernels and creamed corn to the pan.

Add the egg, sour cream and 1 cup (80 g/2 2/3 oz) of the breadcrumbs.

Coat the patties all over with the remaining breadcrumbs.

Shallow-fry the patties for 3–4 minutes on both sides.

Slowly add the olive oil in a thin stream, whisking continually.

WARM CHICKEN SALAD

Preparation time: 15 minutes
Total cooking time: 15 minutes
Serves 4

2 teaspoons cumin seeds
1 tablespoon olive oil
1 red onion, finely sliced
3 cloves garlic, finely chopped
2 teaspoons finely chopped red chilli
1½ teaspoons sweet paprika
600 g (1¼ lb) chicken tenderloins, cut into bite-size pieces
2 tablespoons lemon juice
2 tablespoons chopped fresh coriander leaves
200 g mixed salad leaves
2 Lebanese cucumbers, finely sliced
12 Kalamata olives
2 tablespoons extra virgin olive oil

1 Fry the cumin seeds in a dry frying pan for 1–2 minutes, until fragrant. Remove and set aside. Heat the olive oil in the frying pan, add the onion and cook over medium heat until soft.
2 Add the garlic, cumin seeds, chilli and paprika. Cook, stirring, for 1 minute. Add the chicken and cook for about 5 minutes, still stirring, until the chicken is tender.
3 Remove from the heat and cool slightly. Stir in the lemon juice and coriander, and season to taste with salt. Arrange the salad leaves, cucumber and olives on a serving platter, drizzle with the extra virgin olive oil and place the spicy chicken on top. Serve immediately.

NUTRITION PER SERVE
Protein 35 g; Fat 20 g; Carbohydrate 10 g; Dietary Fibre 5 g; Cholesterol 105 mg; 1520 kJ (365 cal)

Cook the red onion over moderate heat until soft.

Add the bite-size pieces of chicken to the onion and spice mixture.

When the mixture has cooled slightly, stir in the lemon juice and coriander.

CRAB, CHILLI AND CORIANDER NOODLES

Preparation time: 15 minutes
Total cooking time: 10 minutes
Serves 4

2 tablespoons oil
4 spring onions, finely sliced
3 cloves garlic, crushed
2 green chillies, seeded and finely sliced
400 g (12 2/3 oz) fresh crab meat
3 tablespoons lime juice
3 teaspoons grated lime rind
1 teaspoon caster sugar
2 teaspoons sambal oelek
375 g (12 oz) thin dried egg noodles
1 tablespoon sesame oil
2 tablespoons sweet chilli sauce
4 tablespoons chopped fresh coriander

1 Heat the oil in a large frying pan and add the spring onion, garlic and chilli. Cook for 1–2 minutes over low heat, until soft. Add the crab meat, lime juice and rind, caster sugar and sambal oelek. Stir until heated through and season to taste with salt.

2 Cook the noodles in boiling salted water for 2–3 minutes until tender. Drain well and toss with sesame oil.

3 Add the crab mixture, sweet Chilli sauce and coriander to the noodles and gently toss. Serve immediately.

NUTRITION PER SERVE
Protein 25 g; Fat 15 g; Carbohydrate 75 g; Dietary Fibre 5 g; Cholesterol 100 mg; 2340 kJ (560 cal)

COOK'S FILE

Note: You can also use canned crab meat instead of fresh, but you will need 4 x 200 g (6 1/2 oz) cans, as a lot of weight will be lost when it is drained.

Add the crab meat, lime juice and rind, caster sugar and sambal oelek to the pan.

Cook the egg noodles in a large pan of boiling salted water.

After draining, toss the noodles with the sesame oil.

PRAWN AND TOMATO OMELETTE

Preparation time: 15 minutes
Total cooking time: 15 minutes
Serves 6 as a starter

400 g (12²/3 oz) raw prawns
6 eggs, lightly beaten
2 tomatoes, seeded and chopped
3 spring onions, finely sliced
1 tablespoon fish sauce
1 teaspoon sesame oil
3 tablespoons vegetable oil
2 cloves garlic, crushed
2 cm (3/4 inch) piece fresh ginger, finely chopped
1 red or green chilli, finely sliced

1 Shell and devein the prawns, and cut in half lengthways. Combine with the eggs, tomato, spring onion, fish sauce and sesame oil in a bowl, and set aside.

2 Heat a wok over medium heat and add 1 tablespoon oil. Add the garlic, ginger and chilli and cook until softened. Remove from the pan and add to the bowl with the egg mixture, stirring until well combined.

3 Reheat the wok and add a little extra oil. Pour about 1/3 cup (80 ml/ 2³/4 fl oz) of egg mixture into the wok, swirling the pan to make an even omelette (about 10 cm/4 inches round). Cook over medium heat, turning once, for about 2 minutes each side. Remove from the pan and keep warm. Repeat, with the remaining mixture, adding a little more oil as required.

NUTRITION PER SERVE
Protein 20 g; Fat 15 g; Carbohydrate 0 g; Dietary Fibre 0 g; Cholesterol 280 mg; 965 kJ (230 cal)

Cut the shelled and deveined prawns in half lengthways with a sharp knife.

Add the garlic, ginger and chilli to the wok and cook until softened.

Pour 1/3 cup of the egg mixture into the wok and swirl to make an even omelette.

Cook the bacon, chilli, onion and garlic over medium heat, stirring occasionally.

Simmer the sauce until it becomes rich and thick.

Drain and rinse the cooked pasta thoroughly in a colander.

Toss the pasta and sauce together with two wooden spoons.

PASTA ALL' ARRABBIATA

Preparation time: 20 minutes
Total cooking time: 1 hour
Serves 4

4 slices double smoked bacon
2 tablespoons olive oil
4 red chillies, seeded and chopped
2 large onions, finely chopped
3 cloves garlic, crushed
800 g (1 lb 10 oz) very ripe tomatoes, finely chopped
500 g (1 lb) lasagnette pasta
2 tablespoons chopped parsley
grated Parmesan, to serve

1 Chop the bacon. Heat the olive oil in a heavy-based pan and add the bacon, chilli, onion and garlic. Cook the mixture over medium heat for about 8 minutes, stirring occasionally.

2 Add the tomato and 3 tablespoons water to the pan and season to taste with salt and pepper. Cover and simmer for about 40 minutes, or until the sauce is thick and rich.

3 Bring a large pan of water to a rapid boil and then add a little oil. Add the pasta and cook until tender. Drain and rinse thoroughly in a colander, then return the pasta to the pan and keep warm.

4 Add the parsley to the sauce and season again if necessary. Pour the sauce over the pasta, tossing to coat the pasta thoroughly. Serve sprinkled with some grated Parmesan.

NUTRITION PER SERVE
Protein 30 g; Fat 15 g; Carbohydrate 95 g; Dietary Fibre 10 g; Cholesterol 30 mg; 2765 kJ (600 cal)

COOK'S FILE

Note: Good-quality bacon and very ripe, red, full-flavoured tomatoes are essential to the flavour of this dish.

Chilli Sauces

For a condiment with a little extra zing, one of these delicious chilli sauces will spice up an everyday meal or quick snack, and set your next dinner party alight.

ROASTED CHILLI JAM

Remove the seeds and white membrane from 250 g (8 oz) red capsicums and 60 g (2 oz) red jalapeno chillies. Cut into large flattish pieces, and cook, skin-side-up, under a hot grill until the skin blackens and blisters. Place into a plastic bag and set aside to cool, then peel away the skin and discard. Place the flesh in a food processor with 1/4 cup (60 ml/2 fl oz) white vinegar and finely chop. Transfer to a large stainless steel pan and combine with 1/2 cup (125 ml/4 fl oz) white vinegar. Bring to the boil, then reduce the heat slightly and simmer for 5 minutes. Remove from the heat and add 2 cups (500 g/1 lb) white sugar, 1/2 cup (95 g/3 1/4 oz) lightly packed soft brown sugar and 1 tablespoon jam setting granules. Stir until the sugar has completely dissolved, then return to the heat and boil for 5 minutes. Remove from the heat and leave to cool slightly, then carefully pour the chilli jam into hot, sterilised jars and seal tightly. Once opened, keep in the refrigerator for up to 2 months. Serve as a condiment with bread, meats and cheese. Makes about 4 cups.

NUTRITION PER 100 g: Protein 1 g; Fat 0 g; Carbohydrate 55 g; Dietary Fibre 0 g; Cholesterol 0 mg; 910 kJ (215 cal)

TOMATO AND CHILLI SAUCE

Score a cross in the base of 4 ripe tomatoes and place in a heatproof bowl. Cover with boiling water and leave for 10 seconds, then plunge into cold water and peel away the skin from the cross. Roughly chop the flesh and set aside. Heat 1 tablespoon olive oil in a medium pan; add 1 small finely chopped onion and cook for 5 minutes over low heat, or until the onion is soft, stirring occasionally. Add 2 crushed cloves garlic and 2 finely chopped small red chillies and cook, stirring, for 1 more minute. Add the tomato together with 1/4 cup (60 ml/2 fl oz) white wine vinegar and 1 tablespoon brown sugar. Bring to the boil, reduce the heat slightly and simmer for 15 minutes. Remove from the heat and leave to cool, then blend the mixture in a food processor until smooth. Store in an airtight container in the refrigerator for up to 1 month. Serve at the table as a condiment wherever you would normally use tomato sauce. Makes about 1 1/2 cups.

NUTRITION PER 100 g: Protein 1 g; Fat 2 g; Carbohydrate 4 g; Dietary Fibre 1 g; Cholesterol 0 mg; 185 kJ (45 cal)

SAMBAL OELEK

Remove the stalks from 200 g (6½ oz) small red chillies. Combine in a small pan with 1 cup (250 ml/8 fl oz) water and bring to the boil. Simmer, partially covered, for 15 minutes, then cool slightly. Transfer to a food processor, add 1 teaspoon each of salt and sugar, and 1 tablespoon each of vinegar and oil and finely chop. Leave to cool and then place in a sealed container. Keep Sambal Oelek in the refrigerator for up to 2 weeks. Makes about ½ cup.

NUTRITION PER 100 g: Protein 1 g; Fat 4 g; Carbohydrate 3 g; Dietary Fibre 1 g; Cholesterol 0 mg; 205 kJ (50 cal)

CHILLI OIL

Preheat the oven to moderate 180°C (350°F/Gas 4). Spread 200 g (6½ oz) whole red chillies on an oven tray and cook for about 10 minutes, until well roasted but not too black. Cool the chillies slightly and place into a large jar. Pour in 3 cups (750 ml/24 fl oz) of good quality virgin or extra virgin olive oil. Cover with plastic wrap and leave in a cool, dark place for 3 days. Strain the oil into a bottle and discard the chillies. You can dilute the oil to taste with more olive oil, if you find it is too hot. This oil is delicious with crusty bread, salad dressings or to fry onions and garlic for soups, stews and pasta sauce. Makes about 3 cups.

NUTRITION PER 100 g: Protein 0 g; Fat 80 g; Carbohydrate 1 g; Dietary Fibre 1 g; Cholesterol 0 mg; 2915 kJ (695 cal)

CHILLI RELISH

Remove the seeds and membrane from 1 large green capsicum and 1 large red capsicum, and from 3 red or green jalapeno chillies. Cut into large, flattish pieces and cook under a hot grill until the skin has blackened and blistered. Cool in a plastic bag or under a clean tea towel, then peel away the skin and discard. Cut the flesh into thin strips. Combine ½ cup (125 ml/4 fl oz) each of cider vinegar and white wine vinegar in a pan with ½ cup (125 g/4 oz) sugar. Bring to the boil, reduce the heat slightly and simmer until reduced by half. Add the capsicum and chilli strips, 1 tablespoon grated fresh ginger and 2 cloves crushed garlic and simmer for a further 5 minutes. Cool, then stir in 2 tablespoons lemon juice and ½ teaspoon of salt. Transfer to an airtight container and keep, refrigerated, for up to 1 month. Serve with meat or fish. Makes about 1 cup.

NUTRITION PER 100 g: Protein 1 g; Fat 0 g; Carbohydrate 15 g; Dietary Fibre 1 g; Cholesterol 0 mg; 285 kJ (70 cal)

From left to right: Roasted Chilli Jam; Tomato and Chilli Sauce; Sambal Oelek; Chilli Oil; Chilli Relish.

SPICY PORK SALAD

Preparation time: 20 minutes
+ 3 hours marinating
Total cooking time: 15 minutes
Serves 6 as a starter

1 tablespoon oil
500 g (1 lb) pork mince
2 tablespoons fish sauce
1 tablespoon soy sauce
50 ml (1 2/3 fl oz) freshly squeezed lime juice
1 tablespoon soft brown sugar
10 spring onions, finely chopped
3 stems lemon grass, white part only, finely chopped
2 red chillies, seeded and sliced
2 tablespoons each of chopped fresh coriander, mint and parsley
6 lettuce leaves

1 Heat the oil in a frying pan. Add the mince and cook over medium heat until well browned, breaking up any lumps with a fork as it cooks. Remove from the pan and set aside to cool.

2 Combine the fish sauce, soy sauce, lime juice and brown sugar in a bowl. Add the pork mince. Mix in the spring onion, lemon grass, chilli and herbs.

3 Cover and refrigerate for at least 3 hours, stirring occasionally, or overnight. To serve, lay a lettuce leaf on each serving plate and spoon in some of the pork mixture.

NUTRITION PER SERVE
Protein 20 g; Fat 10 g; Carbohydrate 5 g; Dietary Fibre 0 g; Cholesterol 50 mg; 875 kJ (210 cal)

Chop the spring onions, lemon grass, chillies, coriander, mint and parsley.

Break up any lumps of the pork mince with a fork.

Mix in the spring onion, lemon grass, chilli and herbs.

Lightly toast 2 tablespoons of sesame seeds in a dry frying pan.

Cover the strips of beef tightly in plastic wrap and place in the freezer.

Process the onions, spices, sugar, fish sauce and oils into a paste.

Take the beef out of the plastic wrappers and cut into wafer thin slices.

CHARGRILLED LEMON GRASS BEEF WRAPPED IN FLATBREAD

Preparation time: 30 minutes + 5 hours freezing and refrigerating
Total cooking time: 8 minutes
Serves 6

1 kg (1 lb) piece rump steak
6 flatbread (Lavash)
200 g (3 1/3 oz) bean sprouts
3 tomatoes, chopped
1/2 cup (25 g/3/4 oz) chopped fresh mint

Lemon grass Marinade
3 stems lemon grass, white part only, chopped
2 tablespoons sesame seeds, toasted
5 spring onions, chopped
2 cm (1 inch) piece fresh ginger, grated
2 red chillies, seeded
1 onion, chopped
1 teaspoon soft brown sugar
1 tablespoon fish sauce
2 teaspoons sesame oil
2 tablespoons peanut oil

1 Cut the beef into wide strips. Wrap each strip tightly in plastic wrap. Freeze for 2 hours to make the beef easier to slice.

2 To make Lemon Grass Marinade: Combine the lemon grass, sesame seeds, spring onion, ginger, chilli, onion, sugar, fish sauce, sesame oil and peanut oil in a food processor. Process to a paste.

3 Remove the beef from the wrappers and cut into wafer thin slices. Place in a dish with the lemon grass mixture. Cover; refrigerate for at least 3 hours.

4 Brush a heavy-based pan with oil and heat until very hot. Cook the beef briefly, in small batches, until just tender. Place onto the flatbreads; top with the bean sprouts, tomato and mint. Roll the flatbreads up to serve.

NUTRITION PER SERVE
Protein 55 g; Fat 15 g; Carbohydrate 55 g; Dietary Fibre 5 g; Cholesterol 110 mg; 2545 kJ (605 cal)

SEAFOOD SATAY STICKS

Preparation time: 40 minutes
Total cooking time: 15 minutes
Serves 4

Spice Paste

2 large red chillies, seeded and chopped
1 clove garlic, chopped
2 spring onions, finely chopped
1 teaspoon grated fresh ginger
1 tablespoon grated fresh turmeric
1 small tomato, peeled and seeded
1/2 teaspoon coriander seeds
2 tablespoons chopped roasted peanuts
1/2 teaspoon dried shrimp paste
2 teaspoons vegetable oil
1 tablespoon tamarind concentrate
1 tablespoon finely chopped lemon grass, white part only

350 g (11 1/4 oz) skinned boneless snapper fillet
350 g (11 1/4 oz) raw prawns, shelled, tails removed
1 egg, lightly beaten
2 cups (110 g/3 2/3 oz) flaked coconut
4 kaffir lime leaves, shredded
2 tablespoons brown sugar
3/4 cup (185 g/6 oz) whole egg mayonnaise
3 teaspoons grated lime rind
1 tablespoon chopped fresh coriander

1 Soak 6 thick wooden skewers in water for 30 minutes and drain.

2 To make Spice Paste: Coarsely grind the chilli, garlic, spring onion, ginger, turmeric, tomato, coriander, peanuts and shrimp paste in a food processor. Heat the oil in a frying pan and cook the chilli mixture, tamarind and lemon grass for 5 minutes over medium heat, stirring frequently, until golden. Put aside to cool before using.

3 Finely mince the fish and prawns in a food processor. Add the egg, coconut, kaffir lime leaves, sugar and Spice Paste. Season well with salt and pepper; process until well combined.

4 Using wet hands shape 1/4 cup of mixture around the top half of each skewer, then grill or barbecue for 8–10 minutes, turning often, until golden. Combine the mayonnaise, lime rind and fresh coriander in a bowl; serve with the seafood sticks.

NUTRITION PER SERVE
Protein 45 g; Fat 50 g; Carbohydrate 25 g; Dietary Fibre 5 g; Cholesterol 245 mg; 2965 kJ (710 cal)

COOK'S FILE

Note: Try using trimmed stalks of lemon grass instead of skewers—the flavour will be greatly improved.

Cook the Spice Paste in a frying pan until it becomes golden.

Add the egg, coconut, lime leaves, sugar and Spice Paste to the food processor.

Shape the mixture around the top half of the skewers with wet hands.

MARINATED FISH SALAD WITH CHILLI AND BASIL

Preparation time: 30 minutes + marinating
Total cooking time: Nil
Serves 4

500 g (1 lb) firm white fish fillets, skinned
3 tomatoes, diced
3 Lebanese cucumbers, diced
5 spring onions, finely sliced
2 red chillies, seeded and sliced
2 cloves garlic, crushed
1 teaspoon grated fresh ginger
1/2 cup (15 g/1/2 oz) fresh basil leaves, torn
mixed salad leaves, to serve

Marinade
1/4 cup (60 ml/2 fl oz) lime juice
1/4 cup (60 ml/2 fl oz) coconut milk
1 teaspoon salt
1/4 teaspoon cracked pepper

1 Slice the fish into thin strips and place in a glass or ceramic bowl.

2 To make Marinade: Combine the lime juice, coconut milk, salt and pepper in a jug. Pour over the fish. Cover and refrigerate for several hours, turning once or twice, or overnight.

3 Remove the fish from the refrigerator and add the tomato, cucumber, spring onion, chilli, garlic, ginger and basil to the bowl. Mix together well and serve spooned over salad leaves.

NUTRITION PER SERVE
Protein 30 g; Fat 5 g; Carbohydrate 10 g; Dietary Fibre 5 g; Cholesterol 90 mg; 920 kJ (220 cal)

On a chopping board, bunch the 5 spring onions together and finely slice.

Slice the fish fillets into thin strips using a sharp knife.

Pour the marinade over the fish and place in the refrigerator for several hours.

STACKED BEAN ENCHILADAS

Preparation time: 1 hour 30 minutes
Total cooking time: 1 hour 20 minutes
Serves 4

Corn Tortillas

2½ cups (375 g/12 oz) masa harina (see note)
½ teaspoon salt
1⅔ cups (410 ml/13 fl oz) hot water

Filling

2 tablespoons oil
3 onions, finely chopped
4 cloves garlic, finely chopped
4 small red chillies, chopped
1 tablespoon ground coriander
1 tablespoon ground cumin
2 red capsicum, diced
2 green capsicum, diced
2 yellow capsicum, diced
1 cup (200 g/6½ oz) fresh corn kernels
½ cup (125 ml/4 fl oz) vegetable stock
750 g (1½ lb) can red kidney beans, rinsed and drained
1 tablespoon lime juice
3 cups (375 g/12 oz) grated Cheddar
sour cream, to serve

Salsa

2 tomatoes
¼ cup (15 g/½ oz) fresh coriander leaves, chopped
2 red chillies, finely sliced
1 tablespoon lime juice

1 To make Corn Tortillas: Place the masa harina and salt in a large bowl. Add the hot water and mix with your hands to form a soft dough (adding a little extra water if required). Knead gently for 5 minutes. Divide the dough into 12 equal portions; cover with a damp tea towel. Taking 1 portion of the dough at a time, place between 2 pieces of non-stick baking paper. Roll the dough into an 18 cm (6 inch) circle. Stack the tortillas, separating each with greaseproof paper.

2 Heat a heavy-based frying pan or griddle over high heat until very hot, then place a tortilla in the pan. Reduce the heat to medium-high and cook for 30 seconds. Turn over and cook the other side for 1 minute. Turn the tortilla again and cook for a further 30 seconds. Remove and place on a plate. Repeat with the remaining tortillas. Cover with a tea towel to prevent them drying out.

3 To make Filling: Heat the oil in a large, deep heavy-based pan. Add the onion and cook over medium heat for 5–8 minutes, or until golden and translucent. Add the garlic, chilli, coriander and cumin and cook for a further 2 minutes, or until the spices are fragrant. Stir in the capsicum, corn kernels and stock. Bring to the boil, reduce the heat and simmer, covered, for 30 minutes.

4 Preheat the oven to moderate 180°C (350°F/Gas 4). Remove the pan lid and add the kidney beans. Simmer for a further 10 minutes. Add the lime juice and stir through. Season well with cracked black pepper and salt.

5 To assemble the Enchiladas: Lightly brush the tortillas with a little extra corn oil. Place two tortillas on the base of each of two large ovenproof dishes. Cover each with a layer of Cheddar and a layer of bean filling. Place another tortilla on top and repeat the layers of Cheddar and bean filling. Finish with a tortilla and sprinkle with a final layer of Cheddar. Cook for 20–25 minutes, until the Cheddar has melted and the filling has heated through. Serve topped with sour cream and a spoonful of Salsa.

Roll the dough into a circle between 2 pieces of non-stick baking paper.

Cook each tortilla on both sides over medium-high heat.

Simmer the filling mixture over a medium heat for 30 minutes.

6 To make Salsa: Score a small cross into the base of each tomato and place into a heatproof bowl. Cover with boiling water and leave for 10 seconds. Plunge into cold water, then peel away the skin from the cross. Cut in half and scoop out the seeds. Chop the tomato flesh. Combine with the coriander leaves, chilli and lime juice.

NUTRITION PER SERVE
Protein 55 g; Fat 55 g; Carbohydrate 115 g; Dietary Fibre 25 g; Cholesterol 125 mg; 4940 kJ (1180 cal)

COOK'S FILE

Note: Masa harina, the flour used to make the enchiladas, is made from ground corn which has been specially treated. It is available from speciality shops, delicatessens and suppliers of Mexican ingredients.

Add 1 tablespoon of lime juice to the pan and stir it through the mixture.

Layer the tortillas and Cheddar and filling mixture, finishing with a tortilla.

Cover the tomatoes in boiling water for 10 seconds.

CHARGRILLED TUNA WITH CHILLI PASTA

Preparation time: 30 minutes
Total cooking time: 25 minutes
Serves 4

2 teaspoons ground cumin
2 teaspoons ground coriander
1/2 teaspoon ground cinnamon
1/2 teaspoon ground cloves
4 tuna steaks, about 150 g (4 3/4 oz) each

Salad
500 g (1 lb) fresh asparagus
400 g (12 2/3 oz) pasta bows
1 tablespoon oil
1 red capsicum, thinly sliced
1 daikon radish, thinly sliced

Dressing
1/2 teaspoon lemon grass, finely chopped
1/2 teaspoon fresh ginger, finely chopped
1/2 teaspoon sesame oil
2 tablespoons oil
2 tablespoons lemon juice
1 tablespoon light soy sauce
1–2 tablespoons sweet chilli sauce, to taste

1 Combine the spices in a small bowl and dust the tuna steaks lightly.
2 Brush a chargrill pan with oil and grill the tuna for about 2 minutes each side, until lightly browned but still pink in the centre. You can also cook on a barbecue or in a heavy-based frying pan. Slice into bite-sized pieces.
3 To make the Salad: Cut the asparagus into bite-size pieces and cook in boiling water for 2–3 minutes, then drain and plunge into iced water. Drain and set aside. Cook the pasta in a large pan of boiling water until tender; drain. Place the pasta in a large serving bowl and toss with the oil. Add the capsicum, radish, asparagus and tuna; toss to combine.
4 To make Dressing: Whisk the ingredients together until combined and season with freshly ground black pepper. Drizzle over the salad.

NUTRITION PER SERVE
Protein 55 g; Fat 20 g; Carbohydrate 80 g; Dietary Fibre 10 g; Cholesterol 70 mg; 3085 kJ (740 cal)

Dust the tuna steaks lightly with the combined spices.

Chargrill the tuna for 2 minutes on both sides, until lightly browned.

Toss the salad to combine the pasta capsicum, radish, asparagus and tuna.

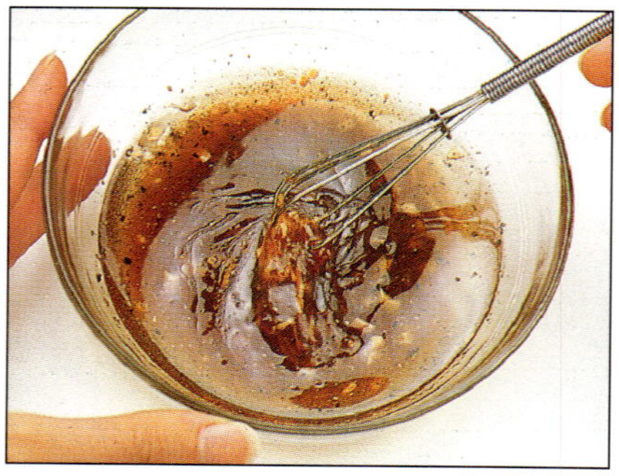

Whisk together all the Dressing ingredients in a bowl.

LEMON CHILLI CHICKEN

Preparation time: 20 minutes
Total cooking time: 35 minutes
Serves 4

2 garlic cloves, chopped
1 tablespoon grated fresh ginger
2 tablespoons olive oil
600 g (1 1/4 lb) chicken thigh fillets
1 teaspoon ground coriander
2 teaspoons ground cumin
1/2 teaspoon ground turmeric
1 chopped red chilli
1/2 cup (125 ml/4 fl oz) lemon juice
3/4 cup (185 ml/6 fl oz) white wine
1 cup (30 g/1 oz) fresh coriander leaves

1 Blend the garlic, ginger and 1 tablespoon water into a paste in a small food processor or mortar and pestle. Heat the olive oil in a heavy-based pan and brown the chicken in batches; remove with a slotted spoon and set aside.

2 Add the garlic paste to the pan and cook, stirring, for 1 minute. Add the coriander, cumin, turmeric and chilli and stir-fry for 1 minute more. Stir in the lemon juice and wine.

3 Add the chicken pieces to the pan and stir to combine. Bring to the boil, then reduce the heat, cover and cook for about 20–25 minutes, stirring occasionally, until the chicken is tender. Remove the lid and cook the sauce over high heat for 5 minutes to reduce it by half. Stir in the coriander and season with salt and pepper to taste. Serve on a bed of steamed Jasmine rice.

NUTRITION PER SERVE
Protein 30 g; Fat 15 g; Carbohydrate 0 g; Dietary Fibre 0 g; Cholesterol 105 mg; 1290 kJ (310 cal)

Brown the chicken in batches to stop the meat from stewing.

Add the coriander, cumin, turmeric and chilli and stir-fry for 1 minute.

Just before serving, stir in 1 cup of fresh coriander leaves.

CHILLI CON QUESO

Preparation time: 15 minutes
Total cooking time: 15 minutes
Serves 4

2 green jalapeno chillies
30 g (1 oz) butter
1 onion, finely chopped
3/4 cup (185 g/6 oz) sour cream
250 g (8 oz) grated Cheddar
corn chips, to serve

1 Roast the chillies by holding them with tongs (one at a time) over a gas flame, until well blackened (or cut the chillies in half, remove the seeds, flatten out and grill until black). Place in a plastic bag and set aside to cool. Scrape away the skin, remove the seeds and finely chop the flesh.
2 Melt the butter in a small pan. Add the onion and cook over medium-low heat for 5 minutes, or until soft and lightly golden. Add the chillies and stir to combine.
3 Add the sour cream and stir until warm and thinned down slightly. Add the cheese and keep stirring until it has melted and the mixture is smooth.

NUTRITION PER SERVE
Protein 20 g; Fat 60 g; Carbohydrate 30 g; Dietary Fibre 5 g; Cholesterol 145 mg; 3030 kJ (725 cal)

Hold the chillies with tongs and roast them, one at a time, over a gas flame.

Add the chopped chilli to the pan and stir until combined with the onion.

Add the cheese to the sauce and stir until it has melted and the mixture is smooth.

CHICKEN AND BEAN CHILLI

Preparation time: 20 minutes + standing
Total cooking time: 50 minutes
Serves 4

1 large onion, chopped
1 tablespoon olive oil
600 g (1 1/4 lb) chicken thigh fillet, cut into bite-size pieces
2 cloves garlic, crushed
2 teaspoons seeded and finely chopped green chilli
1 teaspoon chilli powder
2 teaspoons cumin seeds
1 teaspoon ground coriander
2 x 425 g (13 1/2 oz) can chopped tomatoes
2 teaspoons balsamic vinegar
4 squares dark chocolate, chopped
375 g (12 oz) can kidney beans, rinsed and drained
3 tablespoons chopped fresh coriander

1 Cook the onion in the olive oil until soft. Add the chicken and cook, stirring, over high heat until browned. Add the garlic, chilli, chilli powder, cumin and coriander and cook for 1 minute further.
2 Stir in the tomatoes, vinegar and chocolate. Cover and simmer over low heat for about 40 minutes. Remove the lid for the last 10 minutes of cooking, to allow the liquid to reduce and thicken. Season with salt and black pepper. Leave overnight or for a few hours so the flavours develop.
3 Stir through the red kidney beans and reheat. Just before serving, scatter with the coriander. Serve with rice.

NUTRITION PER SERVE
Protein 45 g; Fat 15 g; Carbohydrate 25 g; Dietary Fibre 15 g; Cholesterol 105 mg; 1710 kJ (410 cal)

COOK'S FILE

Note: You can use 1 tablespoon of soft brown sugar instead of dark chocolate.

Add the bite-size chicken pieces to the pan and stir until browned.

Stir in the tomatoes, balsamic vinegar and dark chocolate.

Add the red kidney beans, stir through and reheat the Chilli.

Chilli Con Queso (top) with Chicken and Bean Chilli

ROASTED TOMATO, CHILLI AND GOATS CHEESE PIZZA

Preparation time: 45 minutes + rising time for pizza dough
Total cooking time: 1 hour 45 minutes
Makes 4 individual pizzas

600 g (1¼ lb) Roma tomatoes, cut in half lengthways and core removed
2 teaspoons olive oil
½ teaspoon salt
⅔ cup (100 g/3⅓ oz) roughly chopped onion
3 cloves garlic, unpeeled
1½ teaspoons seeded and finely chopped red chillies
150 g (4¾ oz) goats cheese
16 Kalamata olives, pitted and roughly chopped
1 tablespoon shredded fresh basil leaves

Pizza Dough
7 g (¼ oz) sachet dry yeast
¼ teaspoon sugar
⅓ cup (80 ml ml/2¾ fl oz) warm water
3 cups (375 g/12 oz) flour
¾ teaspoon salt
3 tablespoons olive oil
¾ cup (185 ml/6 fl oz) water, extra

1 Preheat the oven to slow 150°C (300°F/Gas 2). Place the tomatoes cut-side up on a baking tray. Drizzle with the olive oil and sprinkle with the salt. Cook in the oven for 45 minutes. Add the onion and unpeeled garlic; cook for a further 45 minutes. The tomatoes should be cooked with a few brown roasted edges.

2 Allow the tomatoes and onion to cool slightly, then place in a food processor. Squeeze the garlic out of its skin and add. Process to a thick sauce.

3 To make the Pizza Dough: Place the yeast, sugar, water and ¼ cup (30 g/1 oz) of the flour in a large bowl, stir gently and set aside for 10 minutes, until frothy. Add the remaining flour, salt, olive oil and water. Mix well, then knead for about 15 minutes until the dough is smooth and elastic. Brush with oil and place in a bowl. Cover with plastic wrap and leave in a warm place until the dough doubles in size. This should take about 1½ hours, but will depend on the room temperature.

4 Heat the oven to very hot 240°C (475°F/Gas 9). Knead the dough until it is back to its original size, then divide into 4 equal portions. Press out to make 4 circles, 16 cm (6½ inches) in diameter. Place the circles on two greased baking trays. Stir the chopped chilli through the roasted tomato sauce. Divide among the pizza bases, spreading evenly over each. Leave a 1 cm (½ inch) border around the edge. Crumble the goats cheese over the top of the pizzas. Scatter the pizzas with the chopped olives.

5 Cook in the oven for about 15 minutes, or until the bases are cooked through and crisp. Serve immediately, scattered with basil.

NUTRITION PER SERVE
Protein 20 g; Fat 25 g; Carbohydrate 75 g; Dietary Fibre 10 g; Cholesterol 25 mg; 2625 kJ (625 cal)

COOK'S FILE

Note: Ready-made pizza bases can reduce the preparation time, although you may need to adjust the quantity of topping accordingly.

Cut the tomatoes in half lengthways and remove the cores.

Add the chopped onion and unpeeled garlic to the baking tray.

Gently squeeze the garlic out of its skin into the food processor.

Put the bowl of yeast mixture aside until it becomes frothy.

Place the pizza dough into a bowl and cover with a plastic wrap.

Scatter crumbled goats cheese over the tops of the pizzas.

CALAMARI IN ROASTED TOMATO AND CHILLI SAUCE

Preparation time: 20 minutes
Total cooking time: 2 hours
Serves 4

1 kg (2 lb) egg tomatoes, halved
3 tablespoons olive oil
1/2 teaspoon salt
1 large onion, finely chopped
3 cloves garlic, crushed
1 teaspoon ground cumin
2–3 teaspoons seeded and finely chopped red chilli
1 tablespoon balsamic vinegar
1 bay leaf
1/3 cup (40 g/1 1/3 oz) plain flour
600 g (1 1/4 lb) fresh calamari, cleaned and cut into rings
25 g (3/4 oz) butter
1 tablespoon finely chopped fresh parsley, to serve

1 Preheat the oven to slow 150°C (300°F/Gas 2). Place the halved tomatoes, cut-side-up, on a baking tray. Drizzle with 2 tablespoons of the olive oil and sprinkle with the salt. Roast for 1 1/2 hours, or until they are cooked with brown edges and have lost some of their moisture. Cool slightly then roughly chop. Reserve the juices.

2 Heat the remaining tablespoon of olive oil in a pan and cook the onion until soft and golden. Add the garlic and cumin and cook for 1 minute further. Stir in the chopped roasted tomato and juices, chilli, balsamic vinegar and the bay leaf. Cover and simmer over low heat for 15 minutes. If the sauce seems too dry, add a little water. Remove the bay leaf and season the sauce with salt and pepper.

3 Combine the flour with a good shake of salt and pepper in a plastic bag. Add the calamari rings, a few at a time, and shake to coat with the seasoned flour. Shake off the excess. Melt the butter in a large frying pan, and cook in batches over high heat for 1–2 minutes, or until just white. Stir into the roasted tomato and chilli sauce and sprinkle with the chopped parsley. Serve immediately.

NUTRITION PER SERVE
Protein 30 g; Fat 20 g; Carbohydrate 15 g; Dietary Fibre 5 g; Cholesterol 315 mg; 1555 kJ (370 cal)

Drizzle the tomatoes with olive oil and sprinkle with sea salt before roasting.

Add the roasted tomato, chilli, balsamic vinegar and bay leaf and stir in.

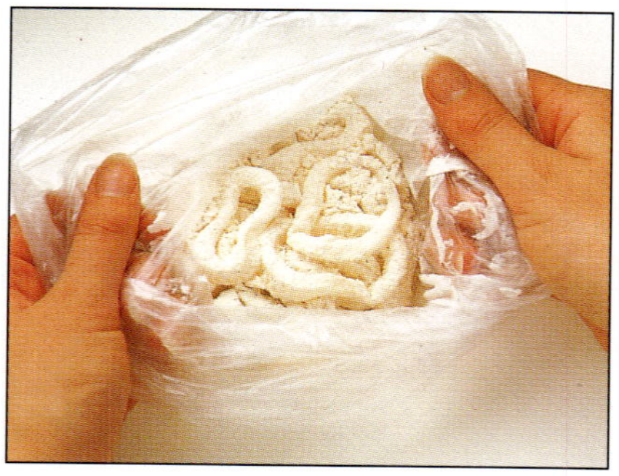

Coat a few calamari rings at a time with the seasoned flour.

THAI-STYLE WHOLE SNAPPER

Preparation time: 10 minutes
Total cooking time: 30 minutes
Serves 4–6

2 garlic cloves, crushed
1 tablespoon fish sauce
2 tablespoons lemon juice
1 tablespoon grated fresh ginger
2 tablespoons sweet chilli sauce
2 tablespoons chopped fresh coriander
1 tablespoon rice wine vinegar
2 tablespoons white wine
600 g (1¼ lb) whole snapper, cleaned and scaled (ask your fishmonger to do this)
2 spring onions, cut into julienne strips

1 Preheat the oven to 190°C (375°F/Gas 5). Place the garlic, fish sauce, lemon juice, ginger, chilli sauce, coriander, rice wine vinegar and wine in a jug and mix together well.

2 Place the snapper on a large piece of foil on a baking tray. Pour the marinade over the fish and sprinkle with the spring onion.

3 Wrap some foil around the fish like a parcel and place in the oven. Bake for 20–30 minutes or until the flesh flakes easily when tested with a fork. Serve immediately with steamed rice.

NUTRITION PER SERVE **(6)**
Protein 20 g; Fat 2 g; Carbohydrate 5 g; Dietary Fibre 0 g; Cholesterol 60 mg; 495 kJ (120 cal)

Mix together the ingredients for the marinade in a jug.

Pour the marinade over the snapper after you have placed it on the aluminium foil.

Cook the fish until the flesh flakes easily when tested with a fork.

PRAWN PARCELS WITH SWEET CHILLI SAUCE

Preparation time: 30 minutes
Total cooking time: 20 minutes
Makes 6

1 tablespoon oil
2 cloves garlic, crushed
1 tablespoon grated fresh ginger
2 tablespoons chopped spring onions
500 g (1 lb) raw prawns, peeled and chopped
1/2 teaspoon fish sauce
1/2 teaspoon sugar
1 tablespoon lemon juice
2 tablespoons chopped fresh coriander
6 whole chives
6 large spring roll wrappers
oil, for deep-frying

Sweet Chilli Sauce
1/2 cup (125 ml/4 fl oz) white wine vinegar
3/4 cup (185 g/6 oz) sugar
4 red chillies, roughly chopped

1 Heat the oil in a frying pan, add the garlic and ginger and cook over low heat for 2 minutes. Add the spring onion and cook for 2 minutes longer. Increase the heat to high, add the prawns and stir-fry for 2 minutes, or until the colour just changes. Be careful not to overcook the prawns or they will become tough once they are deep-fried.

2 Add the fish sauce, sugar, lemon juice and coriander to the pan. Toss through the prawns over the heat for about 1 minute further. Remove the prawns from the heat and allow to cool slightly.

3 Plunge the chives into boiling water for about 10 seconds, then plunge them in iced water to refresh them and dry with paper towels.

4 Divide the prawn mixture into six portions. Place one portion in the centre of each spring roll wrapper. Brush the edges of the wrapper with water and fold to form a parcel.

5 To make Sweet Chilli Sauce: Combine all the ingredients in a small pan and add a pinch of salt. Heat, stirring, without boiling until the sugar has completely dissolved, then bring to the boil, reduce the heat and simmer for 10 minutes. Leave the mixture to cool.

6 Heat the oil in a large deep pan. Deep-fry the parcels one at a time, holding them with tongs for the first few seconds to keep them intact. Cook until they are golden brown. Drain on paper towels, and quickly tie the chives around them. Transfer the cooled sauce mixture to a food processor and mix until the chilli is finely chopped. Serve with the parcels.

NUTRITION PER SERVE
Protein 20 g; Fat 5 g; Carbohydrate 50 g; Dietary Fibre 0 g; Cholesterol 125 mg; 1390 kJ (330 cal)

COOK'S FILE

Note: Keep your face away from the Sweet Chilli Sauce mixture during preparation, as the fumes are very pungent and may irritate the eyes. If you do not feel like making your own, ready-made sweet chilli sauce is available from supermarkets, and Asian food stores.

Hint: If the spring roll wrappers are very thin then use 2 per spring roll.

Storage: Sweet chilli sauce will keep for up to 1 month in a tightly sealed jar in the refrigerator.

Add the chopped prawns to the frying pan and stir-fry for 2 minutes.

Toss the fish sauce, sugar, lemon juice and coriander through the prawns.

Refresh the chives in iced water and dry on paper towels.

Brush the edges of the wrappers with water and fold into parcels.

Hold the parcels with tongs for the first few seconds of frying to keep them intact.

Once the sauce has cooled, pour it into a food processor.

ROASTED CAPSICUM AND SMOKED CHICKEN SOUP

Preparation time: 20 minutes
Total cooking time: 30 minutes
Serves 6–8

4 large red capsicums
1 long green chilli
1 tablespoon olive oil
1 large onion, coarsely chopped
2 cloves garlic, crushed
1/2 teaspoon cayenne pepper
1 teaspoon ground coriander
1 teaspoon ground cumin
2 litres chicken stock
2 cups (315 g/10 oz) smoked chicken, cubed
1/4 cup (7 g/1/4 oz) fresh small coriander leaves
sour cream and tortilla chips, to serve

1 Remove the seeds and membrane from the capsicums and the chilli, and cut into large flattish pieces. Cook, skin-side-up, under a hot grill until the skin blackens and blisters. Remove from the heat, place in a plastic bag and leave to cool, then peel away the skin. Roughly chop the capsicum, and finely slice the chilli.

2 Heat the olive oil in a large pan over medium heat. Add the onion and garlic, and fry for 2–3 minutes. Mix in the cayenne pepper, coriander and cumin and cook for a further 1 minute, stirring constantly. Add the stock, roasted capsicum and chilli and bring to the boil. Reduce the heat and simmer gently for 15 minutes.

3 Remove from the heat, leave to cool slightly, then purée in a blender or food processor in batches until it becomes a smooth soup. Return each batch back to the pan.

4 Reheat the soup over medium heat for 10 minutes. Stir in the chicken and season with pepper. When the soup is hot and ready to serve, add the coriander leaves. Ladle the soup into serving bowls and top each with sour cream. Serve with tortilla chips.

NUTRITION PER SERVE (8)
Protein 35 g; Fat 30 g; Carbohydrate 20 g; Dietary Fibre 5 g; Cholesterol 155 mg; 2120 kJ (505 cal)

When the capsicum has cooled, peel away the blackened skin with you fingers.

Add the stock, roasted chopped capsicum and chilli to the pan.

Reduce the heat and simmer the mixture gently for 15 minutes.

Transfer the mixture to a food processor in batches and purée until smooth.

EGGPLANT, SNOW PEA AND CAPSICUM SALAD

Preparation time: 25 minutes
Total cooking time: 20 minutes
Serves 6

2 red capsicums
500 g (1 lb) slender eggplant
2 tablespoons peanut oil
100 g (3¹/3 oz) snow peas, tops and strings removed

Dressing
1 tablespoon peanut oil
3 cm (1¹/4 inch) piece fresh ginger, grated
2 cloves garlic, crushed
1 teaspoon sesame oil
1 tablespoon balsamic vinegar
1 tablespoon soy sauce
2 red chillies, seeded and sliced
¹/2 cup (125 ml/4 fl oz) chicken stock
1 tablespoon sesame seeds, toasted
2 sliced spring onions
1 tablespoon chopped fresh coriander

1 Remove the seeds and membrane from the capsicums and cut into large flattish pieces. Cook under a hot grill until the skin blackens. Place in a plastic bag and leave to cool. Peel away the skin and slice the flesh.
2 Slice the eggplant diagonally. Brush both sides with oil and grill for about 3 minutes, or until tender; set aside to cool. Place the snow peas in a large heatproof bowl and cover with boiling water. Leave for 1 minute, drain and rinse in cold water; pat dry.
3 To make Dressing: Heat the peanut oil in a small pan and fry the ginger and garlic over low heat for 1 minute. Add the remaining ingredients; simmer for 2 minutes. Remove from the heat and cool.
4 Combine the eggplant, capsicum and snow peas in a serving bowl. Add the Dressing and toss together.

NUTRITION PER SERVE
Protein 5 g; Fat 10 g; Carbohydrate 5 g; Dietary Fibre 5 g; Cholesterol 0 mg; 635 kJ (150 cal)

Cut the capsicums into large flattish pieces with a sharp knife.

Cover the snow peas with boiling water and leave for 1 minute.

Add the remaining Dressing ingredients to the pan.

CRAB WITH LIME AND COCONUT MILK

Preparation time: 45 minutes
Total cooking time: 30 minutes
Serves 6

2 x 1 kg (2 lb) very fresh mud crabs
750 ml (24 fl oz) coconut milk
5 red chillies, seeded and finely sliced
2 tablespoons tamarind concentrate
5 kaffir lime leaves
2 stems lemon grass, white part only, finely chopped
2 teaspoons brown sugar

1 Scrub the crabs to remove any mossy bits. Lift the back apron and remove. Twist off the legs and claws; chop the body into 2 sections with a large cleaver or heavy bladed knife. Wash thoroughly under running water to remove any yellow intestine and feathery gills.

2 Combine the coconut milk, chilli, tamarind, kaffir lime leaves, lemon grass and brown sugar in a large pan. Bring slowly to the boil, stirring occasionally, and season with salt to taste. Add the larger crab pieces, and cook, turning regularly in the sauce, until the shell turns red and the flesh becomes white. Remove from the wok with tongs. Cook the smaller sections and remove. Keep warm.

3 Return the liquid to the boil for 10 minutes, or until reduced and thickened slightly. Serve the crab on a bed of rice and spoon over the sauce. Garnish with extra lime leaves.

NUTRITION PER SERVE
Protein 10 g; Fat 25 g; Carbohydrate 5 g; Dietary Fibre 0 g; Cholesterol 55 mg; 1210 kJ (290 cal)

Use a large cleaver or heavy bladed knife to chop the body into 2 sections.

Cook, turning regularly, until the shell turns red and the flesh turns white.

Boil the liquid for 10 minutes until it has reduced and thickened slightly.

SPICED ROASTED VEGETABLES

Preparation time: 30 minutes
Total cooking time: 55 minutes
Serves 6

3 slender eggplant, halved lengthways
1 leek trimmed and cut into quarters
185 g (6 oz) baby carrots, trimmed and cleaned
1 bulb garlic, cloves separated
3 small red capsicums, quartered
3 small yellow capsicums, quartered
400 g (12 2/3 oz) sweet potato, cut into 1 1/2 cm (5/8 inch) rounds
6 baby new potatoes, halved
1/2 cup (125 ml/4 fl oz) olive oil
1 tablespoon ground cumin
1 tablespoon ground coriander
2 teaspoons fennel seeds
1/2 teaspoon dried chilli flakes
250 g (8 oz) cherry tomatoes
3 tablespoons balsamic vinegar

1 Preheat the oven to moderately hot 180°C (350°F/Gas 4). Place all the vegetables, except the tomatoes, into a large baking dish; drizzle with olive oil. Combine the cumin, coriander, fennel and chilli flakes; scatter over the vegetables. Bake for 30 minutes, or until tender, turning occasionally.

2 Add the tomatoes and roast for 15 minutes. Place the vegetables on a serving plate; reserve any liquid.

3 Combine the vinegar with the reserved vegetable liquid in a small pan. Bring to the boil, then reduce the heat and simmer until reduced by half. Pour the warm dressing over the vegetables and serve immediately.

NUTRITION PER SERVE
Protein 10 g; Fat 20 g; Carbohydrate 35 g; Dietary Fibre 10 g; Cholesterol 0 mg; 1515 kJ (360 cal)

Break open the garlic bulb and separate the cloves.

Combine the cumin, coriander, fennel and chilli and scatter over the vegetables.

Add the cherry tomatoes to the baking dish and continue to roast.

CHICKEN WITH CITRUS LEAVES

Preparation time: 30 minutes
Total cooking time: 45 minutes
Serves 4–6

1 cup (250 ml/8 fl oz) chicken stock
2 teaspoons tamarind concentrate
4 red chillies, seeded
80 g (2 2/3 oz) fresh galangal, roughly chopped
2 stems lemon grass, white part only, roughly chopped
5 spring onions, chopped
5 cloves garlic, roughly chopped
2 teaspoons ground turmeric
3 tablespoons peanut oil
1 1/2–2 kg (3–4 lb) chicken pieces
410 ml (13 fl oz) coconut cream
5 citrus leaves (kaffir or lemon)

1 Heat half the stock in a pan. Remove from the heat and add the tamarind concentrate. Set aside, and allow the tamarind to dissolve.

2 Place the chillies, galangal, lemon grass, spring onion, garlic, turmeric and remaining stock in a food processor and combine well. Heat the peanut oil in a large pan. Add the chilli mixture and fry over low heat for 2 minutes, stirring constantly so the mixture does not stick to the bottom of the pan.

3 Add the chicken to the chilli paste, tossing to coat well. Cook for a further 3–4 minutes, or until the chicken is lightly browned. Stir in the tamarind liquid. Bring to the boil and add the coconut milk and citrus leaves. Reduce the heat and simmer for about 30 minutes, or until the chicken is tender. Remove the chicken and simmer the sauce until it thickens to your desired consistency. Serve the chicken and sauce with steamed rice.

NUTRITION PER SERVE (6)
Protein 65 g; Fat 50 g; Carbohydrate 5 g; Dietary Fibre 5 g; Cholesterol 205 mg; 3000 kJ (715 cal)

Peel and roughly chop the fresh galangal with a sharp knife.

Stir the chilli mixture constantly to stop it sticking to the bottom of the pan.

Add the coconut milk and citrus leaves to the pan.

INDEX

INTERNATIONAL GLOSSARY OF INGREDIENTS

baby squah	pattypan squash
calamari	squid
capsicum	red, green or yellow pepper
caster sugar	superfine sugar
chickpeas	garbanzo beans
chilli	chili pepper, chile
cream	single/light whipping cream
dark chocolate	plain/cooking chocolate
demerara sugar	raw sugar
eggplant	aubergine
egg tomato	plum/Roma tomato
English spinach	spinach
fresh coriander	fresh cilantro
gravy beef	stewing beef
ground almonds	almond meal
Lebanese cucumber	short cucumber
mince	ground meat
mud crab	use any crab
plain flour	all-purpose flour
prawn	shrimp
sambal oelek	chilli paste
soft brown sugar	light brown sugar
spring onion	scallion
snow pea	mangetout
thick cream	double/heavy cream
tomato paste (Aus./US)	tomato purée//double concentrate (UK)
zucchini	courgette

This edition published in 2008 by Bay Books, an imprint of Murdoch Books Pty Limited.
Pier 8/9, 23 Hickson Rd, Millers Point NSW 2000, Australia.

Managing Editor: Rachel Carter **Editors:** Alison Moss, Anna Scobie **Food Director:** Jane Lawson **Food Editors:** Roslyn Anderson, Tracy Rutherford, Jody Vassallo **Creative Director:** Mary Louise Brammer **Designer:** Wing Ping Tong **Recipe Development:** Roslyn Anderson, Amanda Biffin, Rosemary Mellish, Sally Parker, Jo Richardson, Tracy Rutherford, Stephanie Souvlis **Home Economists:** Alex Diblasi, Sharon Glover, Michelle Lawton, Kerrie Mullins, Angela Nahas, Jo Richardson, Alison Turner **Photographers:** Andrew Elton, Ian Hofstetter (cover), Reg Morrison (steps) **Food Stylist:** Georgina Dolling, Michelle Noerianto (cover) **Food Preparation:** Alison Turner, Valli Little (cover)
Chief Executive: Juliet Rogers **Publisher:** Kay Scarlett

The nutritional information provided for each recipe does not include any accompaniments, such as rice, unless they are listed in the ingredients. The values are approximations and can be affected by biological and seasonal variations in food, the unknown composition of some manufactured foods and uncertainty in the dietary database. Nutrient data given are derived primarily from the NUTTAB95 database produced by the Australian New Zealand Food Authority.

ISBN 978 0 68101 349 0
Printed by Hang Tai Printing Company Limited. PRINTED IN CHINA